CW00500132

THE ULTIMATE SEWING MACHINE MASTERY

Tips from a Female Engineer for Flawless Stitches

Katie Matthews

Text and photography by Katie Matthews
Photography by Katie Matthews unless otherwise noted below.
Style photography by Sarah Hurja where stated.

ISBN: 9798871450468

DEDICATION

I dedicate this book to all the creatives who are on their own sewing journeys, to those who sew for their soul and to the wonderful customers I have come to know. Your loyalty is deeply appreciated.

To my dearest Benjamin, who has taught me everything he knows. For your love and patience, but most of all, for believing in me and supporting me through every crazy idea I've ever had. Whose unwavering encouragement and shared dreams have made every step worthwhile.

With gratitude for the love and partnership that enriches my life.

To our six wonderful children, Jamie, Lewis, Lauren, Isabelle, James and Amelia-Rose, who fill my life with joy, wonder and boundless love. Your presence is my greatest inspiration.

This book is for you.

Table Of CONTENTS

UNRAVELLING THE SECRETS OF SEWING MACHINE MASTERY

Behind every flawless stitch, every intricately designed garment and every piece of art brought to life through fabric lies a powerful yet often underappreciated ally—the sewing machine. In the world of crafting, fashion and the handmade, the sewing machine is the unsung hero that transforms the ordinary into the extraordinary.

Welcome to a unique journey through the mechanics and engineering of the sewing machine, guided by a different perspective. As a female engineer deeply passionate about sewing, I've had the privilege of seeing the amazing mechanics and inner workings of these remarkable machines in ways that have only enriched my love for the craft.

My goal with this book is to share the technical insights I have learnt and share the joy that comes from a well-maintained sewing machine.

As a sewing machine engineer and owner of K&B Sewing Machines in Hampshire, UK, I've had the privilege of helping numerous customers with sewing machine issues, from repairs and maintenance to purchasing advice. Having worked on many different types of machines, I have an extensive knowledge to help sewers and relieve frustration.

My involvement in the sewing machine industry continues a family tradition that dates back over 70 years, starting with my partner's grandparents. This legacy began as a way to supplement an extra income after the war when customers would trade sewing machines for window cleaning and odd jobs. This eventually evolved into the ownership of multiple sewing machine shops called J.J & J Read Sewing Machines Ltd, each earning a strong and respected reputation in Hampshire.

Thanks to my partner, Benjamin, I've had the opportunity to acquire traditional skills from vintage sewing machines, skills which have been passed down through the generations. I am very thankful that he has given me the tools, support and teachings he acquired from his time as an engineer.

In the ever-evolving world of sewing, staying up to date with the latest technology is essential. My journey has led me to training with top name brands of contemporary machines. The training emphasised the importance of balancing traditional skills with the technological advancements of modern machines. This is all about using innovation to enhance, not replace, the craft of sewing.

These machines represent a blend of tradition and innovation, and my training has equipped me to harness their potential for the benefit of all sewing enthusiasts.

Why this book?

Perhaps you've encountered the frustration of broken needles, the agony of skipped stitches, or the sudden hiccup in the midst of a creative surge. These are the moments when we wonder, "What went wrong?" In my journey as an engineer and a sewer, I've asked those same questions and sought answers. I've dug deep into the mechanics, played with the tension and demystified the art of the sewing machine. Now, it's my pleasure to pass on the knowledge I've gained, from one passionate sewing enthusiast to another.

This book is not just a technical manual; it's a tapestry woven with threads of passion, precision and creativity. Each chapter is designed to empower you with the skills, insights, and techniques needed to unlock the full potential of your sewing machine. From understanding the fundamental components to troubleshooting common issues, from maintenance routines to needles, we will embark on this journey together.

In the chapters that follow, we will unlock the secrets of sewing machine mastery and discover how proper care and maintenance can elevate our sewing experiences.

Photograph by Sarah Hurja

Whether you're a seasoned pro or just staring your sewing adventure, this book is for you.
Welcome to the wonderful world of sewing machines.

Let's begin...

Photograph by Sarah Hurja

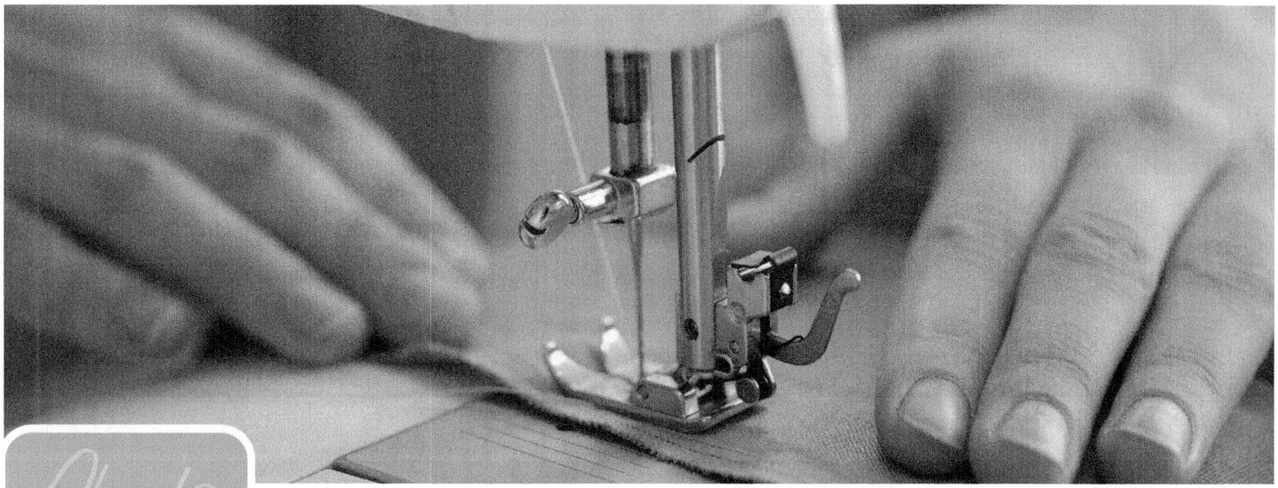

Chapter 01 THE EVOLUTION OF THE DOMESTIC SEWING MACHINE

Charles Fredrick Wiesenthal invented the very first mechanical device for sewing in 1755. This was made up of a double-pointed needle with an eye at one end, which you would use in your hand. Some might say he invented the sewing machine. He was awarded a British patent for this device.

In 1790 the earliest known drawings of a sewing machine were produced by Thomas Saint. These drawings were not made public until 1874 when William Newton Wilson, a sewing machine manufacturer, found the drawings in the London Patent Office. He made small adjustments and built a machine which worked. After much work, in 1790 Thomas Saint invented the very first sewing machine with an overhanging arm, a mechanical feed, a vertical needle bar and a looper. The London Science Museum displays the first model which was taken from Thomas Saint's drawings.

A similar design of the sewing machine was invented by Barthélemy Thimonnier in 1829. The machine used a hook needle and one thread to create a chain stitch. A chain stitch machine creates a distinctive stitch known as a ***chain stitch***. Unlike other sewing machines that use two threads to create a stitch, the chain stitch machine uses a single thread which loops through the fabric to create a chain.

In 1845 American inventor Elias Howe watched his wife sew painstakingly by hand to earn extra money for the family. Howe visualised ways to revolutionise the way she worked. In 1846 Howe was granted a patent for the first practical sewing machine, which featured a lockstitch mechanism. Although he faced initial challenges in gaining acceptance, his invention went on to transform the textile industry and significantly impact the efficiency of garment production.

After Elias Howe's invention of the lockstitch sewing machine, there were many advancements and contributions from other inventors. Isaac Singer was one of these. Isaac improved Howe's design, making the sewing machine more practical and user-friendly. In 1851 Singer patented a machine with a foot treadle for powering the needle. It was widely adopted.

The sewing machine continued to evolve, incorporating various innovations such as interchangeable parts, electric power and automatic features. This played a crucial role in the industrial revolution, transforming the textile and garment industries by increasing efficiency and productivity.

Over time, sewing machines became integral not only to industrial manufacturing but also to households. Singer did extensive marketing and became the first company to introduce credit and payment plans, making the machines affordable for everyone.

A chain stitch machine

Since this time, sewing machines have evolved from basic mechanical sewing machines to computerised models, catering to a wide range of sewing needs and skills.

Take a look at your sewing machine. It is incredible to think how the technology has evolved over the years, yet the principles of the sewing machine remain the same.

Chapter 02

GETTING TO KNOW YOUR SEWING MACHINE

Making friends with your sewing machine and understanding how it works is essential for unleashing its full potential and ensuring a successful and, more importantly, enjoyable sewing experience. Understanding its intricacies allows you to use it correctly, adjust the settings accordingly and troubleshoot any issues that may arise. Further, it empowers you to explore the various stitches, features and functionalities your machine offers, opening up a world of creative possibilities.

Knowing your sewing machine's capabilities enables you to achieve precise and consistent stitches, prevent unnecessary thread jams and maintain good tension. This familiarity not only enhances the quality of your sewing projects but also contributes to the longevity and efficient performance of your sewing machine.

In essence, investing your time in getting to know your sewing machine pays off in the form of improved craftmanship, reduced frustrations and a more satisfying sewing journey.

Sewing machines come in all sizes, makes and models, but the basic anatomy is still the same:

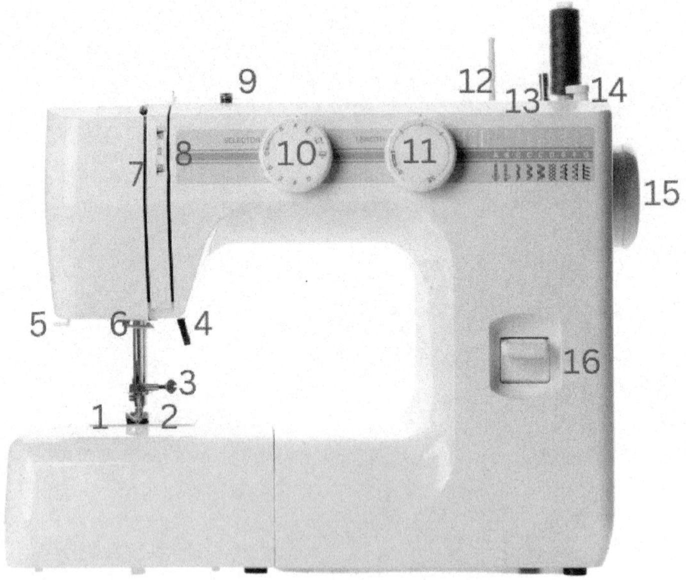

THE BASIC ANATOMY OF A SEWING MACHINE

1. Needle plate
2. Presser foot
3. Needle clamp screw
4. Presser foot lever
5. Thread cutter
6. Thread guide
7. Take up lever
8. Tension dial/tension discs
9. Bobbin tensioner
10. Stitch selector
11. Length dial
12. Spool pin
13. Bobbin winder
14. Bobbin winder spindle
15. Hand wheel
16. Reverse feed lever

Machine Parts and Functions

The needle plate: Marked with guides, the needle plate allows the fabric to smoothly guide through the machine, protects the lower mechanisms and has a hole for the needle to pass through.

Presser foot: Used to put pressure on the fabric and feed the fabric through the machine smoothly, preventing creases.

Needle clamp screw: Holds the needle in place and stops it from falling out.

Presser foot lever: Used for raising and lowering the presser foot.

Thread cutter: Usually situated on the side of your sewing machine, it is a handy cutter to cut your thread tails.

Thread guide: A guide in which the thread sits behind or under, keeping the thread to the correct path to the needle.

Take-up lever: Helps feed the thread and maintain the correct tension when the machine is forming a stitch.

Tension dial: Adjusts the upper thread tension, loosening and tightening the stitch.

Bobbin tensioner: Aids a smooth thread path when winding a bobbin.

Stitch selector: Selects your desired stitch.

Length dial: Selects your desired length of stitch.

Spool pin: Your thread sits on top of the pin, to hold the spool and control thread direction.

Bobbin winder: Winds your bobbin with thread. It is located on the top of the sewing machine near the spool pin.

Bobbin winder spindle: Prevents your bobbin from overfilling with thread.

Hand wheel: The main function is to raise and lower the needle manually and to help with thicker fabrics. It also contributes to winding the thread to the bobbin.

Reverse feed lever: When the lever is pressed, your machine will sew in reverse (backwards). This is used to secure stitches.

Turning on Your Machine

In this section, we'll embark on a hands-on journey with your sewing machine, starting from the moment you turn it on. Proper setup and understanding of the machine's operation are fundamental for your sewing success.

Preparing Your Workspace

Before turning your machine on, ensure your workspace is clean and organised.

Clear any obstructions or debris that could interfere with your machine.

Have your machine on a table at a good working height—the table should be at elbow height to allow you to work with straightened wrists. If you are bending or stretching, adjust the height of your table or chair.

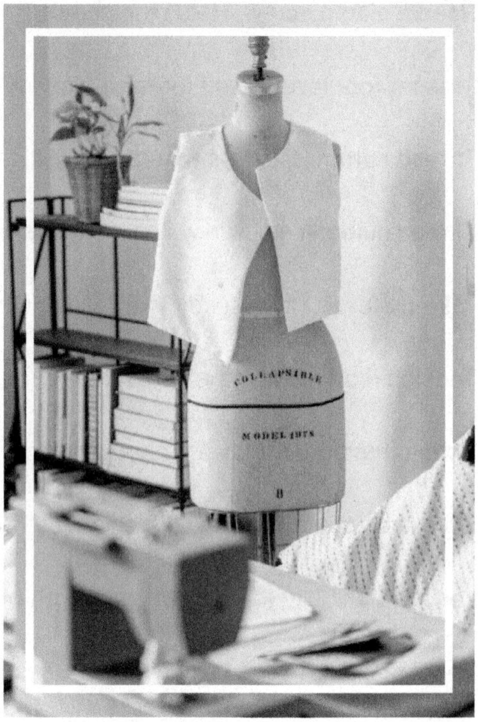

Plugging In and the Power Switch

Locate the power cord and plug it into a suitable socket close to your workspace.

Avoid using extension cords with your machine and overloading the power socket. Turn on the machine and wait for any initialisation processes to complete.

Machine Lights and Display (if applicable)

Many modern sewing machines are equipped with built-in lights for enhanced visibility.

If your machine has a display screen, learn how to navigate it for settings and stitch selection.

Thread Tension and Pressure Adjustments (if needed)

Depending on your machine and the fabric you are using, you may need to make initial thread tension and presser foot adjustments to the amount of pressure the foot places on the fabric.

Refer to your user manual for guidance on these settings.

Safety Precautions

Safety first! Ensure you're familiar with the safety features of your machine.

Be mindful of moving parts and avoid placing fingers near the needle and other moving mechanisms.

Testing Machine Functions

Familiarise yourself with basic machine functions like the hand wheel, which manually moves the needle up and down.

Engage the machine's foot pedal or start/stop function to observe how it controls the sewing speed.

Machine Sounds and Normal Operation

Every sewing machine has unique sounds during operation. Learn to recognise normal sounds, so you can identify unusual noises that might indicate a problem.

Turning Off and Safety

When you're finished sewing, turn off your machine.

Unplug the machine or turn it off, depending on the model. The majority of machines have an on/off switch, but some do not.

Ensure the needle is at its highest point and the machine is in a safe state for storage. Use a dust cover, hard case or bag to store your machine to protect it.

Turning on your sewing machine is the gateway to your creative journey. Understanding its operation and safety measures is important for smooth and enjoyable sewing experiences.

Photograph by Sarah Hurja

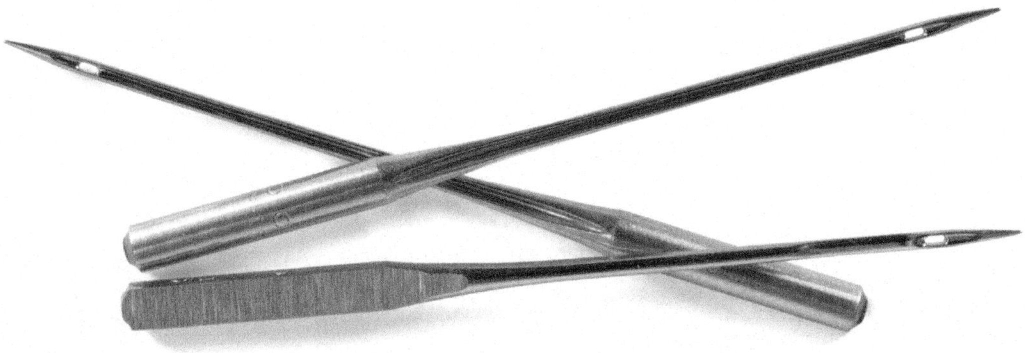

Chapter 03 NEEDLES

Selecting the correct needles for your machine is vital for achieving the best results in your sewing projects. In this section we will explore the considerations when selecting the appropriate needle.

Needle Size

Needle sizes for sewing machines vary based on the type of fabric and thread you are using. Choosing the right needle size is crucial for achieving optimal stitching results.

As a general rule, **the higher the needle size, the thicker the needle.**

NEEDLE SIZES		
European	**American**	**How it's Written**
60	8	60/8
65	9	65/9
70	10	70/10
75	11	75/11
80	12	80/12
90	14	90/14
100	16	100/16
110	18	110/18

European needle sizes: 60–120. Size 60 is the finest needle, and size 120 is thick and heavy.

American needle sizes: 8–19. Size 8 is the finest needle, and size 19 is thick and heavy.

Needle System Numbers

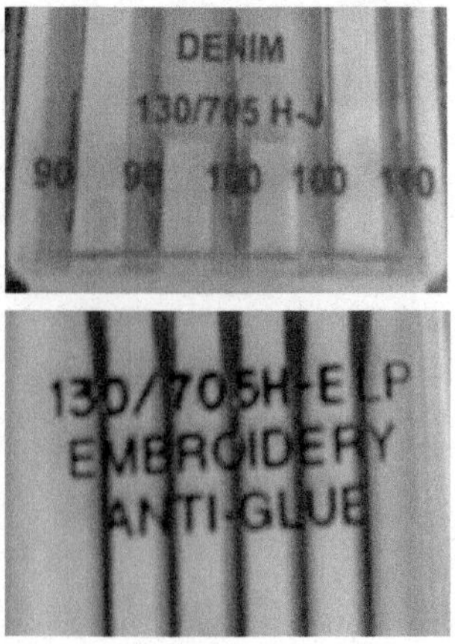

Ninety-nine percent of all domestic sewing machines can take the exact same needle. All of these needles are designed to have the same system number, as they are essentially the same part. The number is displayed on every pack of good-quality, branded needles. However, the confusing part is that each needle manufacturer can have a different system number!

The most common numbers found for domestic machines are 130/705H, HA1, HAx1, 15x1. These numbers refer to the overall dimensions of the needle: length, shank diameter and the flat on the needle shank.

Testing Needle to Thread Size

> ***TOP TIP!***
> *If you are unsure of the size of needle for your thread type, you can do a simple test to select the right size.*

- Cut a metre of the thread you are using in your machine and thread your sewing machine needle at the top of the thread.
- Hold your thread vertically. Watch your needle.
- If your needle drops to the bottom of the thread, your needle is too big.
- If the needle does not slide down the thread and stays at the top, it is too small.
- The correct size needle for your thread will slowly spiral to the bottom.

Understanding the Different Types of Sewing Machine Needles

With so many different needle types on the market, which one do you choose?

Here are the most common needle types:

UNIVERSAL NEEDLES

Universal needles are very versatile. They are suitable for a wide range of fabrics, making them an excellent choice for everyday sewing. They can handle woven and knit fabrics, lightweight and medium-weight materials. They generally feature a slightly rounded, tapered point. This design allows them to pierce a variety of fabrics without causing excessive damage or snags.

They work well with cotton, linen, polyester and blends, making them a great choice for general sewing. Universal needles can be used as twin needle stitching, creating parallel rows of stitches. Check your sewing machine manual for guidance on twin-needle stitching.

Universal needles come in a variety of sizes which you would match according to your fabric type.

BALLPOINT NEEDLES

Ballpoint needles, also known as ***jersey needles***, are a specialised type of sewing needle designed to address the unique characteristics of knit fabrics.

They feature a slightly rounded tip with a groove, rather than a sharp point found in universal needles. This design prevents the needle from cutting or snagging the fibres in knit fabrics.

Ballpoint needles are specifically engineered for knit fabrics, such as jersey, interlock and stretchy materials. They are the perfect choice for sewing stretchy garments like T-shirts, leggings and activewear. They are also suitable for sewing lingerie and swimwear, where delicate fabrics are prevalent.

Choose the appropriate needle size for your knit fabric. These needles allow you to tackle a wide range of fabric projects with confidence.

SHARPS NEEDLES

Sharps needles, sometimes referred to as ***micro-tex*** or ***quilting needles***, are known for their remarkable precision and ability to work with fine and tightly woven fabrics.

They have an ultra-sharp, slender point, making them excellent for delicate fabrics which pierce with minimal damage. The needle point design allows for precise stitching on fine and densely woven materials.

Sharps needles excel with fabrics such as silk, tulle, organza and microfibre. They create precise and clean stitches without causing large holes or puckering.

LEATHER NEEDLES

Leather needles are a specialised type of skin machine needle designed to handle the unique challenges presented by leather and similar heavy materials.

Leather needles have a chisel-like, wedge-shaped point. This design allows them to pierce through leather without tearing or creating overly large holes.

Use a leather needle when working with leather, vinyl, faux leather, suede and other heavy, non-woven fabrics.

Leather needles come in various sizes to accommodate different leather thicknesses and thread types. The appropriate needle should be chosen based on the specific leather and thread used.

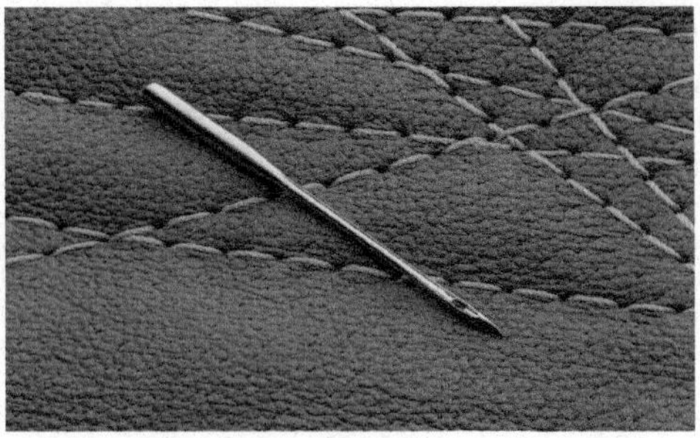

JEANS NEEDLES

Jeans needles are designed to conquer the challenges of denim and other thick, heavy materials.

They have a thick, strong shaft and a very sharp point. This design allows them to pierce through multiple layers of denim at once.

TOPSTITCH NEEDLES

Topstitch needles are versatile and can be used on a range of fabrics, including woven and knit materials. They are primarily intended for topstitching, edge-stitching, and decorative stitching. These needles have a larger eye, so if you are struggling to thread your needle and do not have a needle threader, try one of these in your machine.

They typically feature an elongated eye and a larger groove. This accommodates heavier or decorative topstitching thread, allowing them to pass through the needle more easily.

Pair with a heavier-weight thread for beautiful, prominent, decorative stitches.

METALLIC NEEDLES

Metallic needles are ideal for adding shimmer and shine to your projects, making them suitable for decorative embroidery, quilting and embellishments.

Metallic needles often have a longer eye and a larger groove, much like topstitch needles. This design prevents friction and breakage while ensuring smooth thread flow through the eye.

EMBROIDERY NEEDLES

Embroidery needles are the key to unlocking your creativity in decorative stitching and embroidery projects.

The design, with a slightly rounded point and larger eye, makes them ideal for handling various threads and fabrics. Whether you're monogramming, embellishing or experimenting with free-motion embroidery, these needles will ensure your embroidery work looks professional.

The correct embroidery needle size and thread will enhance your artistic ability to achieve intricate embroidery designs. These needles can be used in a sewing or embroidery machine.

SELF-THREADING NEEDLES

Self-threading needles are available for your sewing machine, but they are only made in sizes 80/12 and 90/14. These typically have a small slit close to the eye of the needle to allow for easy threading.

WING NEEDLES

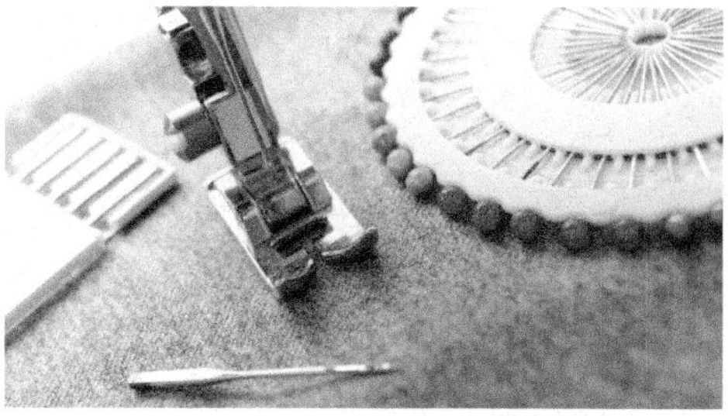

A wing needle is commonly used for heirloom sewing. The needle punches a hole in your woven fabric while the sewing machine stitches around the piercing. This type of stitch is often associated with items such as vintage clothing, handkerchiefs and tablecloths.

Knowing When to Change Your Sewing Machine Needle

Changing your sewing machine needle at the right time is crucial for achieving smooth and high-quality stitches. Here are some key indicators that signal it's time to replace your sewing machine needle:

FREQUENCY

As a general rule, change your sewing machine needle after every 8–10 hours of sewing. This helps to maintain consistent stitching quality.

DULL OR BENT NEEDLE

If your needle becomes dull or bent, it's time to replace it. Bent and dull needles can cause skipped stitches, fabric damage and damage to your machine.

A bent needle is the most common cause of skipped stitches and poor stitch quality. I see this problem in my workshop on a daily basis. If you are experiencing these issues, re-thread your machine and pop a new needle in.

This is a photograph of a needle plate, which has been struck continuously by bent needles. The thread on this sewing machine was breaking and the stitches were uneven due to the damage.

FABRIC SNAGS OR RUNS

If you notice snags, runs or puckering in your fabric, your needle may be the culprit. A damaged needle can catch and damage the fabric.

THREAD BREAKAGE

Frequent thread breakage is a sign that the needle is not smoothly guiding the thread. A new needle can resolve this issue.

AUDIBLE CHANGES

Unusual sounds like clunking or clicking during sewing can indicate a needle problem. Replace it to eliminate the noise.

UNEVEN STITCHES

If your stitches are inconsistent in length or tension, the needle is most likely responsible. Installing a needle can help achieve balanced stitching.

SKIPPED STITCHES

Skipped stitches are a clear sign that your needle is not piercing the fabric as it should. A fresh needle can remedy this issue. If you have changed your needle and are having further issues, check that your thread is of good quality.

SPECIALITY PROJECTS

When transitioning from one project to another, especially if you are switching fabric types or needle requirements (for example, from denim to silk), change the needle to match the new project's needs.

LARGE PROJECTS

For extensive or long sewing projects, it's a good practice to change your needle partway through to maintain stitch quality.

TOP TIP:
By paying attention to these indicators and replacing your sewing machine needle as needed, you'll ensure that your machine operates smoothly and your stitches remain of the highest quality. This proactive approach to needle maintenance not only preserves fabric but also prevents potential machine damage down the line.

Chapter 04

THREAD

Choosing the Appropriate Thread for Your Sewing Machine

Selecting the right thread for your machine is a crucial decision that directly impacts the quality of your stitches and the longevity of your machine. In this section, we'll delve into the considerations when choosing thread:

Thread Weight

Different threads come in various weights or thicknesses, often indicated by a number on the spool (for example, 30, 40, 60). Choose a thread weight suitable for your machine. Heavier threads may require adjustments to your machine's tension settings.

Thread Fibre Type

Threads are available in a range of materials, such as cotton, polyester, silk and speciality threads like metallic or monofilament. Consider the fabric you'll be sewing and select a thread that complements it. For example, cotton thread pairs well with cotton fabrics.

Matching Bobbin and Upper Thread

Ideally the thread in the bobbin should match the thread used in the upper part of the machine—not in colour necessarily, but in thread weight and brand. Consistency in thread type and weight promotes even tension and smoother stitching.

Thread Colour

Thread colour should harmonise with your fabric, especially where you don't want stitches to be visible. Opt for a colour that blends seamlessly. For a contrast or decorative stitch, why not try a variegated thread to add a unique design touch?

Specialised Threads

Some projects may benefit from using a specialised thread, for example, metallic. Although these types of thread can be trickier to work with, there are many tools you can use to make your stitches more successful.

TOP TIP!
Try lubricating your thread before stitching or using a spool net on your thread reel. Some branded machines sell lubrication units you can fit to your machine. This goes on the thread path, so your thread is lubricated before it gets to the needle.

Thread Storage and Quality:

Always buy the best thread you can afford. Using a top-quality thread which is lint free will be kinder to your machine and produce beautiful stitches without frustration.

Properly store your threads away from direct sunlight and humidity to maintain their quality.

Avoid using old threads from your grandmother's sewing box in your sewing machine. Over time, thread fibres break down, causing the thread to snap and shred at the needle.

TOP TIP!
Just by changing your thread to one of high quality, you will notice a big difference in your sewing machine's performance.

Experiment and Record

Don't hesitate to experiment with different thread weights on fabric scraps. Keep a record of the thread types and settings that produce the best results for your future reference.

Choosing the appropriate thread for your sewing machine is a foundational step in achieving professional and consistent results. By understanding the nuances of thread weight, fibre type, and colour, you'll be better equipped to select the perfect thread for each project, ensuring a smooth and enjoyable sewing experience.

Loading Your Sewing Machine Thread

Loading the thread into your sewing machine is a fundamental step that sets the stage for your sewing project. In this section, we'll explore the intricacies of thread loading, from winding the bobbin to threading your needle.

Selecting the Right Bobbin

Understand the type of bobbin your machine uses (for example, plastic or metal, flat or curved).

Ensure the bobbin is compatible with your machine model. If in doubt, check your sewing machine manual. There are hundreds of bobbin types on the market which claim to fit your machine, but many do not.

Always go by manufacturer recommendations and use genuine bobbins. An incorrect bobbin can cause wear on your machine, tension issues and irregular stitches.

Thread Selection

Choose the appropriate thread for your bobbin. Refer to the section in this book on thread weight.

Placing the Thread

Place the thread you are using on the spool holder. If your thread is cross wound onto the spool in the manufacturing process, it will glide off the spool more smoothly when using the horizontal spool pin. If, however, it is wound onto the reel straight (left to right) then it will be better to have it on your vertical spool pin. This allows the thread to gently unravel smoothly without pulls.

Many sewing machines have a second spool pin, sometimes removable. Have a look at your machine to see if you have this option.

Spool Caps

Spool caps serve two purposes. First, the cap holds the thread on the spool pin and prevents the thread from rattling or falling off. Second, it ensures the upper thread does not snag on the reel as it is coming off, and it stops obstructions on the thread path.

An obstruction along the upper thread path will cause you problems. This could be a ball of tangled thread, a build-up of lint or a small cut in the sewing machine's outer casing.

When you purchased your machine, you might have noticed that there were several sizes of spool caps. The reason for this is that different thread companies produce different sizes of spools in a variety of shapes and sizes.

Selecting the Correct Spool Cap for Your Thread

Match the spool cap to the size of the thread spool you are using, and change it accordingly when changing thread.

> ***TOP TIP!***
> *The general rule is that the spool cap should be slightly larger than the plastic end of the spool itself.*

Why? Well, if you examine a spool cap, you will notice that it is made from smooth plastic. Compare this to the end of the spool itself—it is a rougher plastic, often with imperfections that can potentially snag the thread and cause problems with our stitches.

When using a spool cap, the thread will gently guide over the smooth surface of the cap rather than the end of the spool.

The top picture shows the correct spool cap for the size of thread, allowing the thread to gently guide over the cap smoothly. The bottom picture shows the same size thread reel using a large spool cap. This is the wrong size cap for this thread. There is a greater chance that your thread will tangle when coming off the reel.

Here are some examples of what your spool caps may look like.

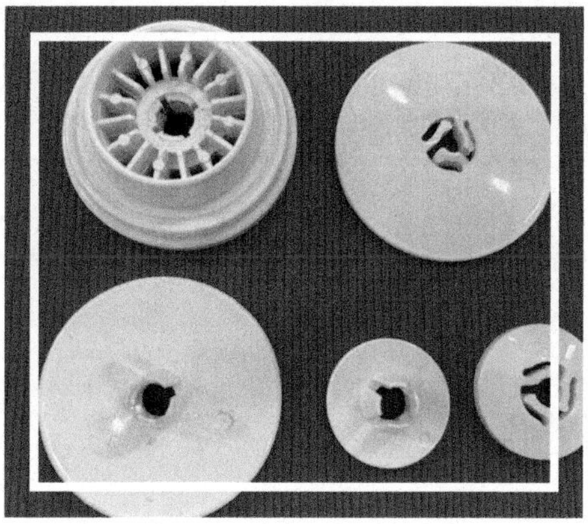

Threading the Upper Thread

Examine your machine's threading diagram in your user manual and follow the thread path guide carefully.

> ***TOP TIP!***
> *Always thread your sewing machine with the presser foot up. This allows the thread to guide through the top tension discs. If you were to thread with the foot down, you would have no upper tension.*

The majority of machines thread in this particular way:

- Down through the tension discs and up through the take-up lever. Ensure your thread is properly seated in this lever. Then down towards the needle.
- Before threading your needle, make sure you have threaded through any thread guides along the path.
- Thread the needle from front to back. Some machines can be threaded from left to right, so check your manual to make sure.
- Use a needle threader if your machine has one. It is a good idea to practice using your threader. The needle threader is a lever that is pulled down to the needle. It turns, and a small piece of wire with a hook on it will catch the thread and pull it through the eye of the needle, leaving a small loop at the back. Pull the loop, and your needle will be threaded. This can take a little practice, but once you are familiar with using it, it will save you lots of time.

Final Checks and Preparing to Sew

TESTING THE UPPER TENSION

Once you have threaded the upper part of your machine, put your presser foot down and try to pull the thread through the needle. Is there resistance? If so, your thread is correctly threaded through the tension unit inside the machine.

On older models and some industrial machines, the tension unit is located on the outside of the machine casing. This will look like two metal discs. When the presser foot is raised, the discs will open, and when it is lowered, the discs will close, giving you upper tension.

BRINGING UP THE BOBBIN THREAD

With some modern sewing machines, you do not have to bring the bobbin thread up from underneath, so you may not need to do this step.

- Lower the needle down, turning the hand wheel towards you. This will bring up the bobbin thread, which you can then pull to the surface.
- Test your stitches on a fabric scrap before sewing your project. This helps you to see if your machine is performing correctly without ruining your fabric. If you have any issues, re-thread your machine and follow the steps again.

Your machine is now properly threaded and you are ready to start stitching.

Loading the thread correctly sets the foundation for successful sewing. With your bobbin and upper thread in place, you're equipped to embark on your sewing project.

Photograph by Sarah Hurja

Chapter 05

BOBBINS & BOBBIN CASES

Winding the Bobbin

Select your bobbin and thread your machine through the correct thread path. This process can vary for each machine. Refer to your manual for your machine's correct path. The thread may have to go through several guides and a tensioner for this.

> ***TOP TIP!***
> *If you cross-thread your thread at the tensioner, you will get an even fill on your bobbin.*

When filling your bobbin, always refer to your sewing machine manual. Following the correct guides and thread path on your machine will ensure your bobbin fills tightly enough and evenly. If your bobbin is incorrectly wound or unevenly filled, it may cause you to have irregular stitches and tension problems. If in doubt, re-wind your bobbin.

That Pesky Tail of Thread

After you have filled your bobbin, you may notice that you are left with a short tail of thread coming from the hole. This little tail, if not removed, will catch the thread going around the bobbin case which makes the stitch inside your machine and will result in problematic stitches.

There are two ways it can be removed. You could cut the tail short so it doesn't get in the way, or when you wind the bobbin, hold onto the tail of thread close to the bobbin while winding, until it breaks. Continue to wind the bobbin.

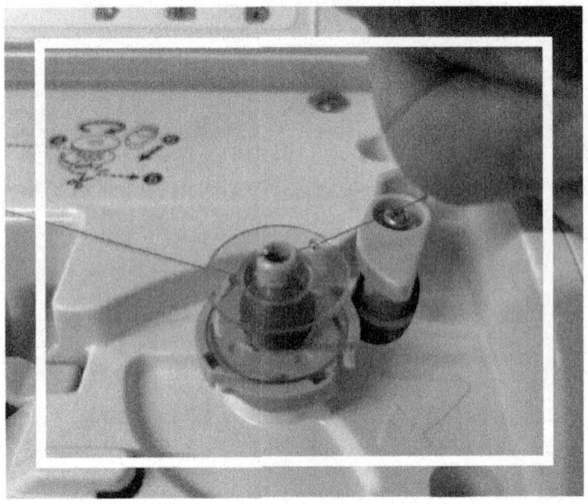

Pictured here, you can see the tail of thread left on the bobbin which could cause potential problems.

Pictured above are just a few of the various types of bobbins on the market.

Using the correct bobbin in your sewing machine is crucial for several reasons.

- **Compatibility:** Different sewing machine makes and models require a specific bobbin to ensure it fits the bobbin case and aligns with the machine's mechanisms. If your bobbin fits in the bobbin case, this does not mean it is the correct one. Every bobbin has a slight difference. This could be in shape or size.
- **Tension control:** Using an incorrect bobbin can cause tension issues, resulting in loose or uneven stitches.
- **Stitch quality:** The correct bobbin ensures that your sewing machine produces high-quality stitches. The wrong bobbin can cause thread jams, skipped stitches, thread breakage and other irregularities in your sewing.
- **Damage prevention:** Using the wrong bobbin can damage your sewing machine and your bobbin case. For example, a metal bobbin in a plastic bobbin case can cause wear to the case.

To ensure that you are using the right bobbin for your machine, refer to your manufacturer's guidelines in your manual.

Bobbin Cases

Bobbin cases come in all shapes and sizes. The most common removeable cases can be found below.

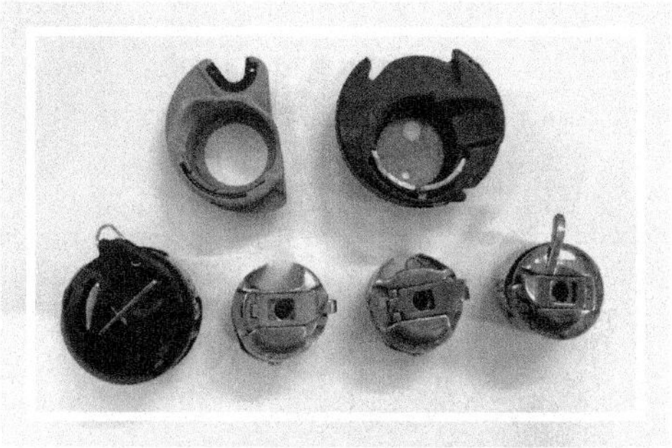

Bottom-loading bobbin case (You can remove the bobbin case to place the bobbin in.)

Top-loading bobbin case. (The plastic bobbin case is situated under the needle plate, and the bobbin is placed into the case.)

There are many other types of sewing machine systems, but these are the most common. Your bobbin could be placed into the back of your machine or the side, depending on the age, make and model.

Bobbin Cases for Bobbin Work

If you want to use yarn, decorative thread, wool or fine ribbons, you can use these materials with a bobbin work case. This kind of bobbin case is perfect for those materials that can't be threaded through a needle on your sewing machine. Several manufacturers make these bobbin cases to fit different models of machines.

An example of a bobbin work case

Chapter 06

TENSION

Mastering the skill of setting your tension takes practice and patience. Balancing the tension between the upper and lower thread is essential for achieving flawless stitches. With experience, you'll become better at fine-tuning your sewing machine's tension, ensuring your stitches remain consistent. It is a good idea to have your tension calibrated by a trained technician or engineer to begin with until you get to grips with it.

In this section we will explore the key aspects of thread tension.

Balanced Tension

The correct tension is vital for securing stitches that look the same on both sides of the fabric. When balanced, the upper and lower threads will lock within the fabric layers.

Tension Disc System

Sewing machines have tension discs through which the upper thread passes. Tension adjustments are made by changing the pressure on these discs.

Upper Thread Tension

To increase upper thread tension, turn the tension dial to a higher number. To decrease tension, turn it to a lower number.

The ideal setting varies depending on your project and fabric. Some machines have built-in automatic tension. This changes automatically itself, and you do not have to calibrate it.

Bobbin Thread Tension

If your tension is tight on top and you have used the dial with no success, it is time to look at your lower tension. Do the next step if absolutely necessary. If it is not handled with care, you may find yourself taking the machine to your local sewing machine shop for a tension reset.

- Adjusting bobbin thread tension is typically done by altering a small screw on the bobbin case.
- Make a minute adjustment as needed to match the upper thread tension a 1/4 turn on the screw at a time.
- After each adjustment, stitch a sample, review and then tweak some more. Notice how the stitch changes. Ideally, stitches should look the same on both sides of the fabric.

Loops or Puckering

Loose upper tension can result in loops on the underside of the fabric.

Tight upper tension can cause puckering or gathering on the fabric's surface.

Manual Reference

Your sewing machine's manual often provides guidance on adjusting tension for specific fabrics and threads. Consult it for reference when working on new projects.

If you do not have the original manual with your machine, take a look online, as most manufacturer's manuals can be downloaded.

TO DO

TASK!

Select the zigzag stitch on your machine and stitch a line of stitches. As you are moving down the line, slowly change the top tension on your machine. Stop and mark next to the stitches what top tension number you are using.

Record and evaluate which part of the line looks the best, on the front and back side of your fabric. This will help you to understand your settings and the correct tension for good stitches.

Don't worry if you can't get a good tension at first on your machine. It can take a lot of practice to get the adjustment right.

The sample below shows the top side of the fabric. This is a good tension.

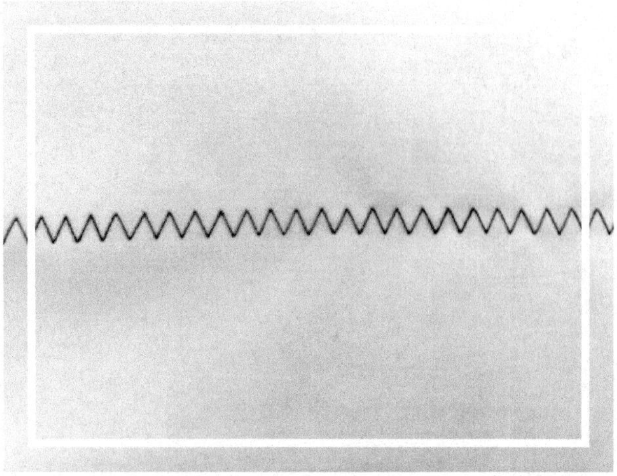

This sample shows an incorrect tension on the top side of the fabric. The upper tension is too tight, pulling up the lower thread. Therefore, the top tension needs to be loosened slightly or the bottom bobbin case tension tightened.

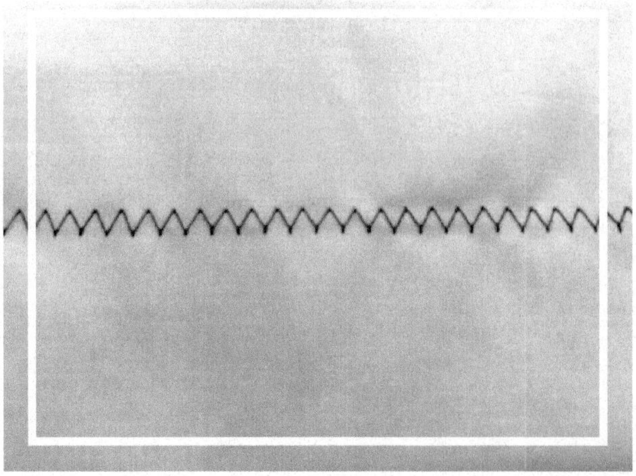

Chapter 07

THE PRESSER FOOT

The presser foot is a fundamental component of your sewing machine, playing a crucial role in achieving sewing success. In this section, we will explore the key aspects of the presser foot and its impact on your sewing outcomes:

Fabric Control

The presser foot holds the fabric in place during sewing, ensuring it doesn't shift or wrinkle.

Stability is important for achieving even and precise stitches.

Fabric Feeding

The fabric is fed through the machine with a part of the machine known as the *feed dog.*

The combination of the presser foot and the feed dog working together pulls the fabric through the machine evenly.

Presser Foot Types

Different presser foot types are designed for various sewing tasks. For example, there are ***standard presser feet, zipper feet, buttonhole feet*** and many more. Choosing the right foot for your project enhances your ability to control the fabric and create specific techniques and stitches.

Speciality Presser Feet:

Speciality presser feet, such as ***walking feet*** or ***quilting feet***, are designed for specific sewing techniques.

They help manage multiple layers of fabric or unconventional materials, ensuring even stitching.

Stitch Quality

The presser foot's role in holding the fabric steady and feeding it accurately influences the quality of your stitches.

Proper alignment and fabric control lead to even and neat seams.

Seam Allowances

The presser foot often includes markings that assist in maintaining consistent seam allowances.

These guides ensure that your seams are straight and match your project's requirements.

Foot Pressure

Some sewing machines allow you to adjust the foot pressure. This may be a small circular dial on the top of your machine, or if your machine is electronic, it may be in the system settings.

Increasing or decreasing pressure can be beneficial when working with different fabric thicknesses.

Zips and Buttonholes

Specialised presser feet for zips and buttonholes simplify these otherwise tricky tasks. Throughout my time as an engineer, I have noticed that approximately 70 percent of people do not know how to use this feature.

TASK!

Familiarise yourself with your presser feet for zips and buttonholes. Play with your machine settings and refer to your manual if needed. Can you use this feature confidently?

Raising and Lowering:

The ability to raise and lower the presser foot is necessary for inserting or removing fabric from under the needle.

This feature allows you to manoeuvre fabric with ease.

TOP TIP!

Regularly maintain your presser foot to prevent lint and debris from affecting its performance. Check for any marks, scars or damage. You can clean it with an old, dry toothbrush. A well-maintained pressure foot ensures smooth fabric control.

The Perils of a Satin Stitch Foot

Throughout my time as a sewing machine engineer, I have noticed a recurring issue with the satin stitch foot being used for the regular straight stitch and zigzag. If you turn the foot over, it has a tunnel which creates extra room for bulkier stitches. If this foot is used for regular sewing it can cause tension issues. Check your foot. Do you use this one?

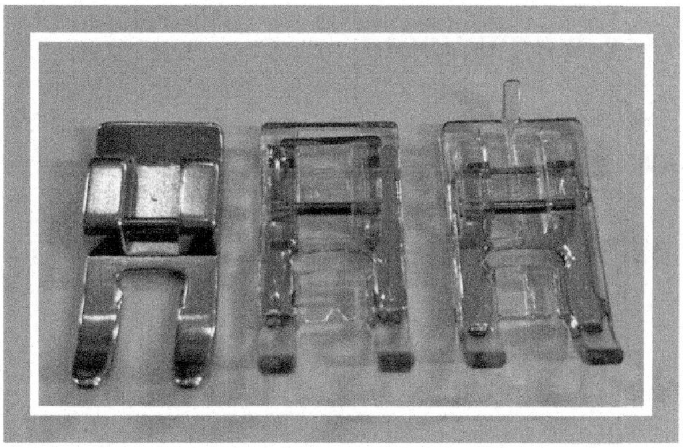

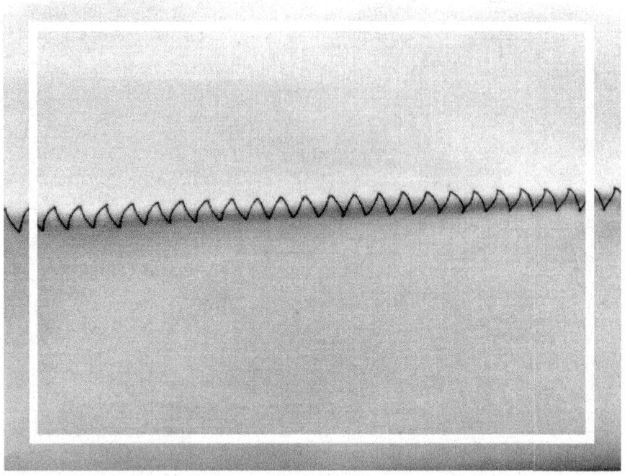

The tunnel effect from using a satin stitch foot

The correct foot for regular sewing is the straight stitch or zigzag foot. This is smooth underneath to allow the foot to glide across the fabric. This will also keep stitches flat and neat while giving the correct tension.

Notice the difference between these feet and the satin stitch foot.

Walking Foot

A ***walking foot*** is beneficial when sewing several layers of fabric together. It stops the fabric layers from moving, which may cause your fabric to crease up or slide. The feed dog teeth pull the fabric through from the bottom, and the teeth on the walking foot pull it through from above, resulting in an even feed.

This works particularly well when quilting, handling slippery and thick fabric and sewing plaids.

Interchangeable Soles

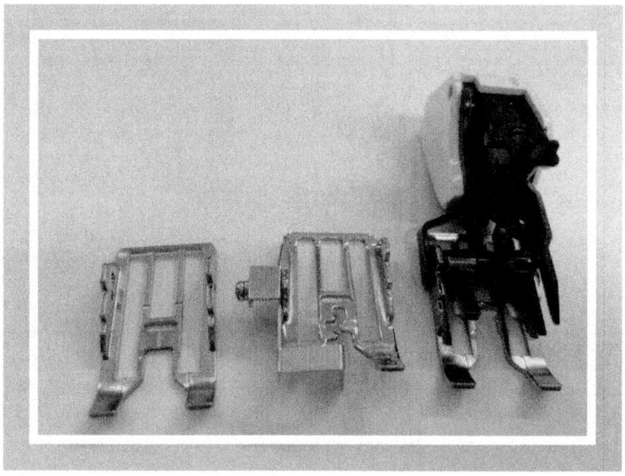

Walking feet can come with different attachments called ***soles***. These are interchangeable depending on the project you are working on.

Sewing sole: This works well when sewing leather or velvet and for matching plaids. Quite often there are marks on the foot for seams and cornering guides. These can be found in 1/4" and 1/8" markings (left sole, pictured above).

Quilting sole: The ***quilting sole*** is best used for machine quilting. This has an open toe (a gap at the front) which helps visibility when quilting. It may also provide 1/4" and 1/8" markings. The back of the quilting sole is designed to reduce drag on the quilt and give an even feed from the top and bottom layers (as seen on the walking foot above).

Edge stitching sole: Use this for stitching along the edge of the fabric or for in-the-ditch stitching. This foot will have a handy built-in guide (centre sole).

Patchwork or 1/4" Foot

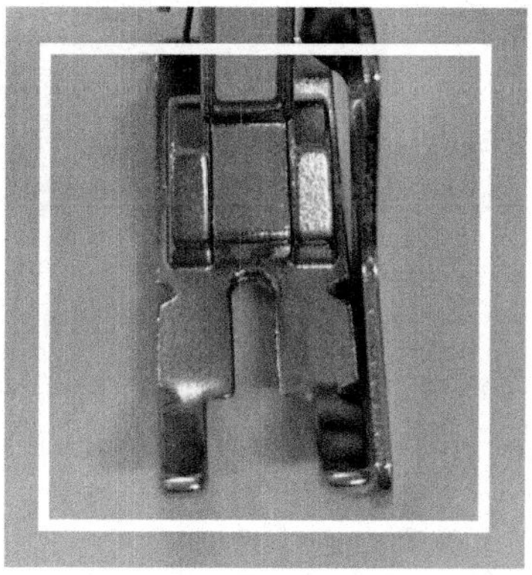

The *patchwork or 1/4" foot* is the quilter's friend and the most useful foot for the perfect measurement. These feet commonly will have three markings or notches. These markings are made in 1/8" increments. The distance from the needle to the edge of the foot is 1/4".

Some manufacturers' 1/4" foot will come with a guide. The guide is intended to ride on the outside edge of the seam to give you an accurate seam allowance. When using the 1/4" foot (with or without the guide), make sure that your needle is set to the ***centre straight*** stitch setting.

Edge Stitch Foot/Stitch in the Ditch

The *edge stitch foot/stitch in the ditch foot* helps you sew a perfectly straight stitch in relation to the fabric or seam. It is great for tucks, hems, seams and fine edge work when using decorative trim, ribbon or lace. With the needle position to the left, it will give a 1/8" seam. Set your machine to ***straight stitch*** to use this foot. If the needle is in the centre position, you will be sewing in the ditch.

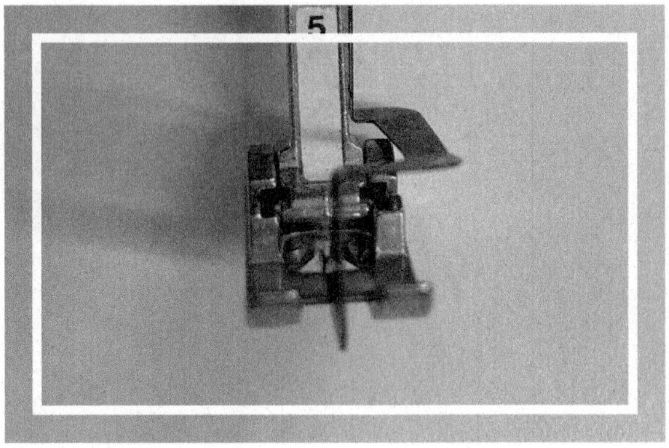

Often, this foot is used to stitch in the ditch when quilting. The guide will run along a seam between two pieces of fabrics, creating a subtle line of stitching to hold the two pieces together securely.

Your edge stitch foot can also be used for binding the edge of quilts, placemats and other projects. It is a versatile foot which has many uses, giving you a professional finish.

Overcast/Overlock/Overedge Foot

The majority of machines will have a stitch you can use with the ***overcast/overlock/overedge foot***. The styles may vary depending on the manufacturer, but they will work in the same way.

It is designed to finish the raw edges of your fabric—a little like an overlocker would, but it will not cut the fabric. It works by having a bar in the centre which wraps the thread around the edge of the fabric as you stitch.

Line your fabric up against the guide and select an ***over-edge stitch*** or a ***zigzag***. As a general rule, the stitches that are formed moving forwards on the sewing machine are best for light- to medium-weight fabrics, and the stitches that move back and forth are best suited to medium-heavy weight.

> ***TOP TIP:***
> *Experiment with your fabric and see which stitch will give you the best finish.*

There are many other ways to use this foot. You can create a rolled hem by using a zigzag stitch, pressing the hem to curl up and over, and feeding it through, so the fabric curls around the centre bar.

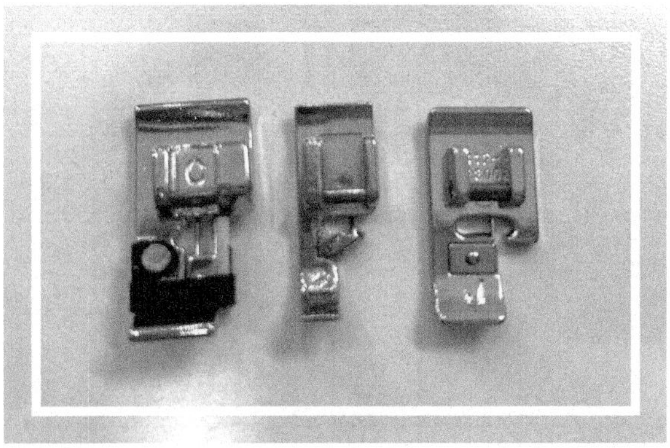

Blind Hem Foot

The ***blind hem foot*** is used to create a stitch that is barely visible from the front side of the fabric. This is well suited for sewing garments, hems and curtains. The guide on the foot can be used for joining edges, pin tucks and top stitching. Some guides on a blind hem foot can be adjusted.

Free-Motion or Darning Foot

Free-motion or darning feet come in varying shapes and sizes. Some can be mainly plastic and other solid metal. Yours may have a spring on it to help regulate the tension on heavier-weight fabric. It may have an oval at the foot, or it could be open for better visibility. Whichever foot you have, they all work in a similar way.

Using your machine to do free-motion embroidery is much like drawing with your sewing machine. The freedom of movement allows you to go in any direction you wish. This works well if you put your fabric into a hoop, keeping the fabric taut, or alternatively use a stabiliser or lightweight interfacing on the back to prevent puckering.

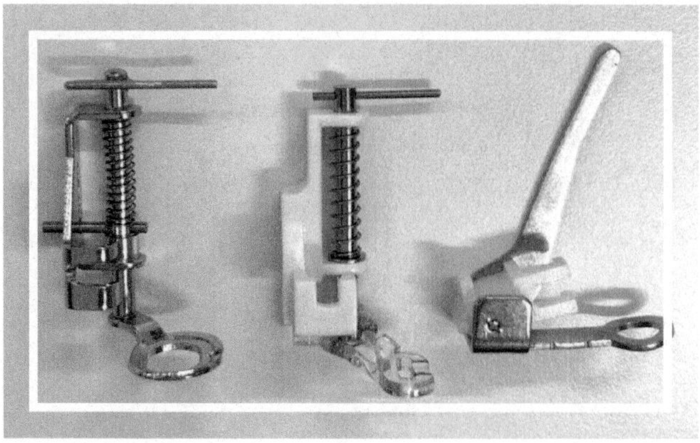

Lowering the Feed Dog for Free-Motion Work

To use the free-motion/darning foot, you will need to drop the feed dog on the machine. This is the metal teeth that come up through the needle plate which feeds the fabric through. Some machines may come with a small plate to cover the feed dog, and on others the feed dog can be dropped out of the way.

The foot allows you to sew freely and not be restricted to just going forwards and backwards. It is commonly used for free-motion embroidery and quilting. There are only two stitches which can be used with this foot, *straight stitch* and *zigzag*.

Zipper Foot

The *zipper foot* features a narrow design that allows the needle to stitch close to the edge of the fabric, making it easier to sew along the teeth of the zip. This foot can also be used for anything that you need to get close to the edge of.

Stitch Regulator

Some manufacturers have produced a foot called a ***stitch regulator***. This regulates the stitches to keep them neat, consistent and of equal length. This is almost impossible to achieve with a regular free motion or darning foot. The foot is plugged into the machine and works with the machine to speed up or slow down the stitches as you move the fabric. This foot works well for free-motion quilting.

Teflon Foot

A *Teflon foot* is a non-stick foot which is used to sew tricky fabrics that may not feed smoothly through a sewing machine, for example, leather, vinyl, plastics and slippery silks. Using the foot will prevent puckering and will keep layers even.

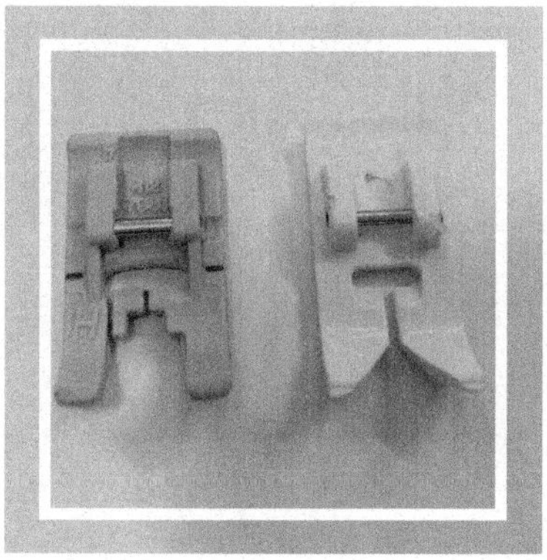

Roller Foot

If you are working with fabrics that are harder to sew, the *roller foot* may help glide the fabric under the foot. The roller on the foot helps to reduce friction, making it easier to glide with the fabric as the feed dog pulls it underneath. The foot can be used with fur, velvets, PVC and leather.

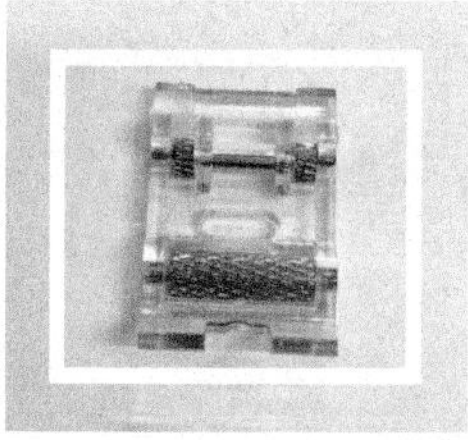

Photograph by Sarah Hurja

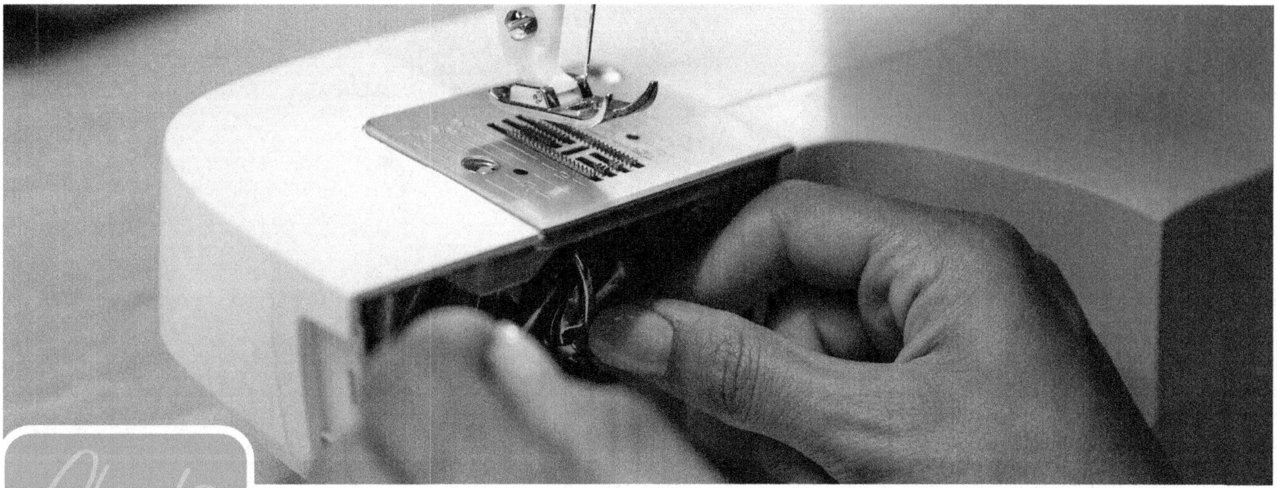

Chapter 08

STITCH PLATES

A *stitch plate* covers the feed dog on your sewing machine. It can also be known as a *needle plate*. Some sewing machine stitch plates are interchangeable. Changing your stitch plate gives better results depending on your project.

For example, a *straight stitch plate* will have a single round hole for the needle to go through. This stops the fabric from being pulled into the machine. This is particularly useful when using lighter-weight fabrics.

Each machine will have a stitch plate designed for the widest stitch available on your model. Depending on your machine's maximum width setting, these come in various sizes, differing per model and manufacturer.

Photograph by Sarah Hurja

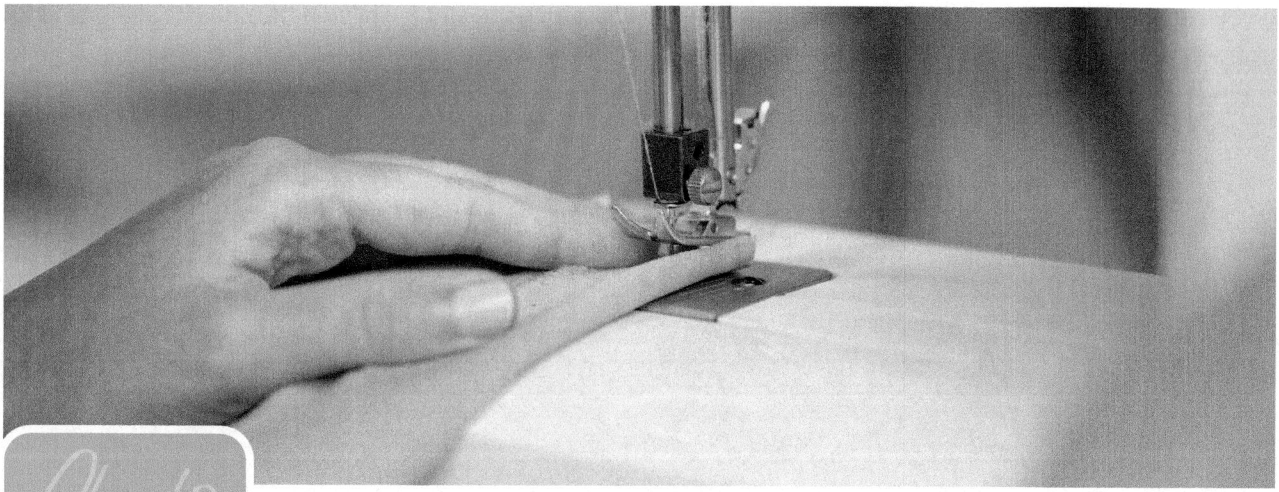

Chapter 09

STITCHES

How Is a Stitch Formed on a Sewing Machine?

A sewing machine creates a stitch by the upper and lower threads working in tandem. The needle moves downwards, piercing the fabric. The upper thread, from the spool, forms a loop around the bobbin case. As the needle rises, a small hook catches the upper thread and intertwines with the bobbin thread, creating a secured stitch on the fabric. The continuous interplay of threads form the stitches as you sew.

During this next chapter we will discuss the basic utility stitches on your sewing machine and what they can be used for.

Please note:
You may find that the name of the stitch varies depending on the manufacturer of your machine.

STRAIGHT STITCH

The most basic and most commonly used stitch on our sewing machines is the ***straight stitch***. This is used for general sewing, top stitching and securing seams. Adjusting the length of your straight stitch will make your stitches longer or shorter. You can customise this depending on what fabric you are using and its purpose.

If you have a width control on your sewing machine and you widen the stitch while on the straight stitch setting, this will make a zigzag line of stitches. For perfectly straight lines, set your width to 0.

Straight stitch is also good for free-motion work, tacking, darts and more.

> ***TOP TIP:***
> *As a guide, set your machine length between 2.5 and 3.5 for general sewing. Some sewing machines will have a pre-set length, but this can be altered if desired.*

The straight stitch can also be used for top stitching and can be done with your regular straight stitch foot.

The ***triple straight stitch*** is depicted on your machine as three broken lines. This stitch uses a two-step-forwards and on-step-back pattern. It can be known as a ***back stitch or triple stretch stitch.*** It is used to sew very strong seams in stretchy fabrics. It can also be used to sew in difficult areas like an arm hole on garments and is great when used for top stitching.

A ***securing straight stitch*** can be found on some modern machines. It secures the beginning and end of the seams and can be used with all types of fabric. It is particularly useful when sewing long lines of straight stitching. This will look like a line with a triangle on each end. Check your manual to see if your machine does this stitch.

ZIGZAG STITCH

The ***zigzag*** is a versatile stitch and is used for finishing raw edges to prevent fraying, seam finishes, buttonholes, satin stitching and more. For some sewing techniques using this stitch, it can be helpful to use your satin stitch foot. A ***satin stitch*** is a closely spaced zigzag stitch. To make the satin stitch, adjust the stitch length between 0.5 and 2.0, depending on the weight of the thread being used.

The width of the zigzag can be adjusted using the length and width settings on your machine if you have them.

A multi-stitch zigzag, sometimes known as a ***three-point zigzag***, makes three short stitches whereas the regular zigzag makes only one; this works great as a stretch stitch.

The ***lightning stitch*** is another great zigzag stitch. This looks like an angled zigzag at a short length or a lightning bolt. It is most commonly used when working with knit fabrics, as they tend to stretch. This allows the fabric to stretch, but the stitches won't.

BLIND HEM STITCH

A ***blind hem stitch*** consists of a straight stitch on the right-hand side along the hem, with a single zigzag stitch on the left. The zigzag catches a small amount of fabric, leaving a neat finish which is barely visible.

This is a useful stitch when sewing two pieces of folded edges together, as the thread is barely visible from the outer side. It can be used when sewing hems and attaching pockets, facings and trims to garments. This stitch can be used anywhere where you want a neat, finished edge.

OVERLOCK/OVEREDGE STITCH

The ***overlock stitch*** is designed to finish seams and prevent fraying on the edge of fabrics. This stitch works well on stretchy and woven fabrics, and using this stitch will prevent seams from popping open when pulled.

It is a combination of the straight stitch and the zigzag stitch. It sews backwards and forwards in a straight line, but between every set of straight stitches, it sews a zigzag. If used correctly, this will resemble the same stitch made when using an overlocker.

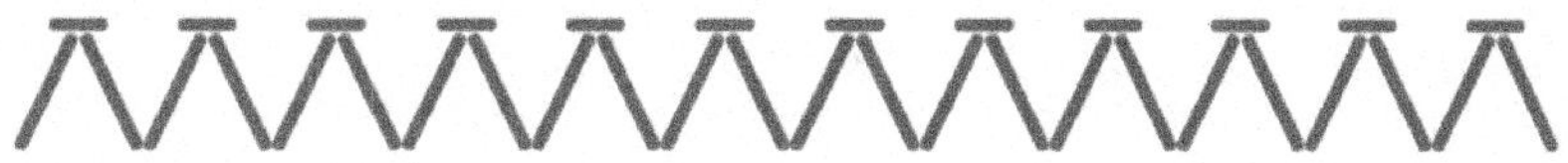

HONEYCOMB STITCH

If you are attaching elastic or stretch lace to your project, opt for the ***honeycomb stitch***. It will give strength to the fabric, and when stretched, the stitches will not break. The stitch zigzags back and forth and is useful for hems on sportswear garments and smocking.

BLANKET STITCH

A popular use for the ***blanket stitch*** is applique. When a shape is placed on top of another piece of fabric, the stitch will secure the two pieces together, giving a decorative finish. It can create pretty edges on the edge of blankets or join two pieces together. It also prevents fraying. Quite often, it is used when making felt items and stitched toys.

DECORATIVE STITCHES

Decorative stitches are one of the most versatile stitches on a sewing machine, but may be rarely used. Some people refer to decorative stitches as "embroidery stitches". While some of them do look like works of embroidery, in the sewing world embroidery stitches are made using an embroidery machine and hoop. Decorative stitches are those that can be sewn like a regular straight stitch on a sewing machine.

Below are some exciting new ways to use the decorative stitches on your machine:

- Stitch in the ditch—add areas of interest to your quilt by using a decorative stitch.
- Instead of sewing bindings with a straight stitch, try using a decorative stitch. This method can be super quick and look amazing.
- When couching, instead of using a standard straight or zigzag stitch, try using a decorative stitch to attach fibres and ribbon.
- Use decorative stitches to make machine lace fabric on water-soluble fabric or on top of your fabric. Make your own trim and add beads!
- Add interest to garments on hems or seams.
- Use decorative stitches to add surface texture and decoration to your fabric.
- Make a faux ribbon effect by adding a couple of rows on either side of a straight stitch.
- You can make jewellery, hanging mobiles and more using decorative stitches on your machine. Stitch on water-soluble fabric and wash away the base.
- Use decorative stitches for applique.

TOP TIP:
Play with your stitches and try adding some decoration to your next make!

There are many other stitches that can be found on a sewing machine. This is not an exhaustive list, but it is the most commonly used.

STRETCH STITCH BALANCE ADJUSTMENTS

If stretch stitch patterns are uneven when you sew on a particular fabric, adjust them with the ***feed balancing dial***. This can be located at the front or back of your machine, but not all sewing machines have this feature. It is a circular-shaped dial with a line, which can be adjusted with a flat screwdriver. Some modern machines will have this adjustment on the screen. Consult your manual if you are unsure.

If your pattern is too drawn out, correct the stitch by turning the dial in the direction of the minus (-).

If patterns are too compressed together, turn the dial in the direction of the plus (+).

This feature can be particularly useful when you are having issues with your buttonhole balance.

Photograph by Sarah Hurja

Chapter 10 MINI PROJECT: MAKE A STITCH BOOK

A good way to familiarise yourself with your sewing machine is to make a stitch book. This not only helps you choose the right stitch for future projects but teaches you how to use your machine while making something useful! You can refer to your stitch book at a later date when you need help in choosing the right stitch for your project.

What you will need for a felt stitch book:

- 3/4 pieces of felt or fabric, depending on the number of stitches your machine has
- Your chosen thread (Use different colours to make it more fun and interesting.)
- Your sewing machine
- A drink of your choice and a couple of hours to spare

Instructions for Felt Stitch Book

Start by cutting the cover to your desired size. Fold it in half. This will be your front cover. Put this to one side. You could make this from felt or fabric. (If you are using fabric, you will need some interfacing and two pieces of fabric of the same size to make the cover.) Place right sides together, add interfacing, and stitch around the edge, leaving an opening to turn your fabric. Turn the fabric and top stitch around the edge to give a neat finish.

Next, cut the two pages from felt to size to fit neatly inside the cover. Mark a centre line in the middle. (Use a heat removable pen, as this will be on show.)

Once you have done this, you can start stitching!

It is a good idea to do one stitch per line. Work your way through each stitch on your sewing machine, until you fill your book. You can also add buttonholes any other features your machine has.

It is your book, so get creative!

When you have filled your book, it's time to decorate the front cover. If your machine has writing, then you could add some text, appliqué or beads. Make it your own.

Lay your pages out in your desired order and stitch a centre line down through the middle of your book to secure them together.

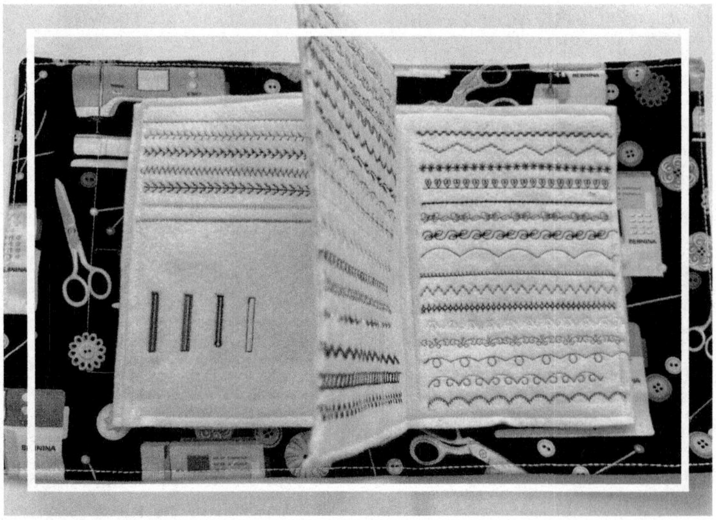

I have used fabric for my cover and felt for the inside pages. You can make your stitch book however you wish.

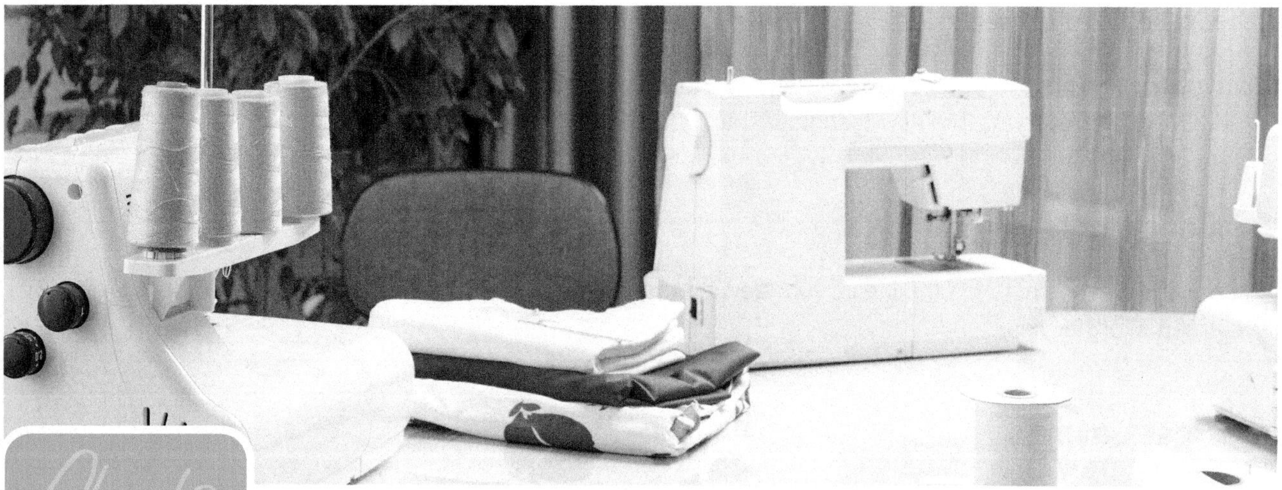

Chapter 11

THE JOY OF A WELL-MAINTAINED SEWING MACHINE

Owning and maintaining a sewing machine in top condition brings a wealth of joy and benefits to your sewing experience. In this section we will explore the many reasons why a well-maintained machine is a source of delight.

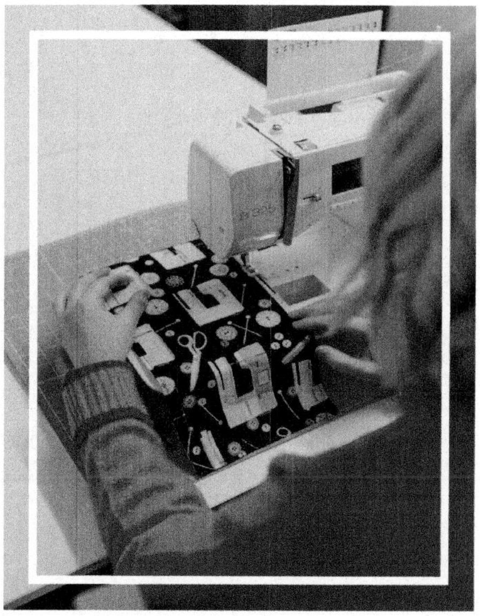

Photograph by Sarah Hurja

Consistent Results

A well-maintained machine produces consistent, high-quality stitches on every project. Your stitches are even, strong, and precisely where they should be, giving you confidence in your work.

Fewer Frustrations

When our machine is not performing as it should, we can get frustrated with dealing with thread snarls, jams, or skipped stitches. A smoothly operating machine makes sewing more enjoyable and stress-free. How many times have you been frustrated and ended up having to walk away from your machine?

Creativity Unleashed

When your machine is in good condition, you can focus on your creativity rather than troubleshooting machine issues. You'll be free to explore new techniques and take on more challenging projects.

Longevity

Proper maintenance extends the life of your sewing machine. You'll enjoy years of productive use, making your investment worthwhile.

Cost Savings

Regular maintenance can prevent major breakdowns and costly repairs. Your machine will require fewer visits to an engineer, saving you money.

Enhanced Learning

When your machine continually performs at its best, you can focus on learning new techniques and improving your skills. The joy of continuous improvement becomes a driving force in your sewing journey.

Photograph by Sarah Hurja

Chapter 12 MAINTENANCE

Regular maintenance of your machine not only prolongs its life, but also contributes to the quality of your sewing. By dedicating time for cleaning and oiling your machine and following the manufacturer's guidelines, you'll enjoy a machine that continues to deliver consistent results.

Looking after your machine may seem like a daunting task at first, but over time you will become familiar with your machine, and it will become a good habit.

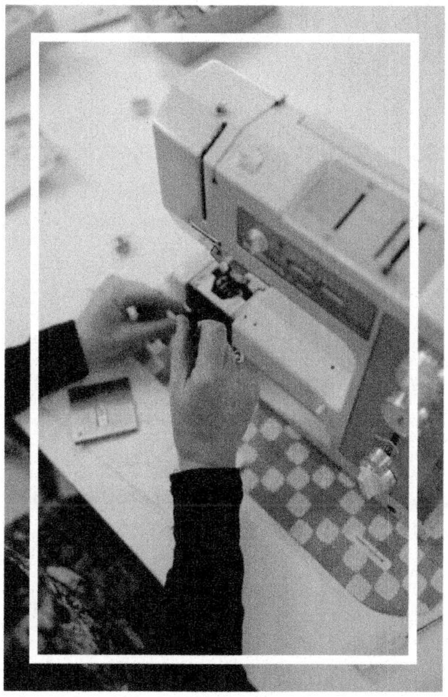

Photograph by Sarah Hurja

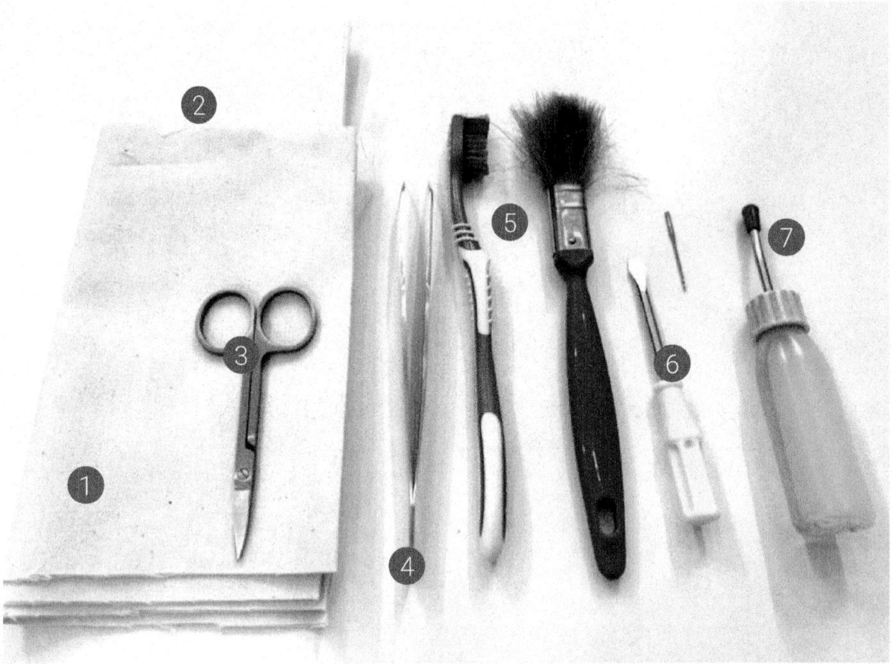

BASIC MAINTENANCE KIT TO CLEAN YOUR MACHINE

1. Scrap fabric
2. Lint-free cloth
3. Small scissors
4. Tweezers
5. Toothbrush or dry paintbrush
6. Screwdriver for needle plate
7. Sewing machine oil

Start by turning off your sewing machine.

Cleaning:

- Regularly clean your sewing machine, including the bobbin area and feed dog. On some bottom-loading machines, you can remove the hook to clean it. This is the piece of metal that looks like a half-moon (found in bottom-loading machines).
- Remove the needle plate from your machine, as dust and lint can build up underneath. (You may have to use a small screwdriver to do this.)
- Use a toothbrush or paintbrush to collect lint and dirt. Remove any loose threads with tweezers.
- With your presser foot raised, use a folded piece of fabric and gently slide the fabric through the tension discs. This will remove any build-up of lint or snapped thread.

I would recommend cleaning your machine every couple of months at a minimum. Depending on usage and fabric used, you may find you need to do this more regularly.

TO DO

TASK:
Take a look at your sewing machine. When was the last time you cleaned it? Follow the cleaning instructions to start a good routine today.

Oiling Your Machine:

- Follow your machine's manual for oiling instructions.
- Use high-quality sewing machine oil and apply it sparingly to the recommended points on your machine.
- Some machines which run at high speed may require a specific oil, for example, Velocite Oil. Refer to the manufacturer's guidelines for the type of oil required and the oiling points.
- Some manufacturers may say not to oil your machine. You should follow these guidelines, as you may cause potential harm to your machine by putting oil near electronics or sensors.

> *TOP TIP!*
> *A sewing machine is very similar to a car. If we left our car without using it for a long period of time, it would not work. A sewing machine is the same. Take good care of it, clean it, oil it and have it serviced regularly.*

Always sew onto a piece of scrap fabric before starting your project to remove any excess oil.

Bobbin Care

- Keep your bobbins clean and free of lint. Replace them if they become worn or damaged.
- Make sure your bobbin case is in good order and functioning smoothly. Also see the "Selecting the Right Bobbin" section.

Needle Replacement:

- Change your needle regularly, especially after heavy use or when it becomes dull or bent.
- Use the right type and size of needle for your project.

Threading Review:

- Periodically review your machine's threading, ensuring that the upper and lower threads are correctly threaded.
- Incorrect threading can result in sewing problems.

Bulbs

Always use a low-wattage, anti-vibration bulb designed for sewing machines. Modern sewing machines are often fitted with LED bulbs. These will need to be changed by your sewing machine engineer, as they will often be replaced with new wiring and a new mini circuit board.

If your sewing machine is a basic model or an older machine, it may take a screw-in bulb or have a bayonet fitting. If you are able to change this yourself, always check that your sewing machine is unplugged and wait for the bulb to cool down, as they can get very hot.

Regular Servicing

A regular full service for your sewing machine is necessary not only to prolong its life, but also to address issues that may not be apparent during routine cleaning. Take your machine to a sewing machine engineer or technician annually, regardless of whether your machine has been used or not.

TOP TIP!
There is never a good time to give up your beloved machine for a routine service, but don't leave it until problems arise. If you are a daily sewer, consider purchasing a smaller backup sewing machine to use.

It is important to build up a good relationship with your sewing machine engineer or technician; you never know when you may need them. Always take your machine to a qualified person and read reviews before deciding on where you take your machine. Also ask the technician questions. You must feel comfortable leaving your machine with them.

Perhaps set up some other tasks that you can do while you are waiting for the work to be done, for example, cutting out a pattern or hand stitching.

Storage

- Store your sewing machine in a clean, dry place, preferably in a protective case or cover.
- Keep it away from direct heat sources like sunlight or next to a radiator.
- Avoid extreme temperature fluctuations.

FACT:
A high-quality sewing machine came into my workshop for a full service after it was purchased brand new only six months previously. When I removed the cover, it was seized with rust and damp. The customer kept her machine in a summer house outside, which she had set up as a sewing room. Sadly, this voided the warranty on her machine, it was not performing well and it could not be repaired.

Always think about where you are storing your machine when it is not in use.

Automatic Thread Cutters

Some modern machines have built-in thread cutters. It is possible that if not correctly maintained, they can break, bend or get stuck, causing your machine internal damage.

When you press the button to cut your threads, a small arm will reach across under your needle plate and pull the thread over to a small, sharp blade. This will then cut your thread. Sometimes a tail of thread can get caught in the cutter, and if not kept clean and free of thread, it can build up and stop the cutter from working altogether.

When you are cleaning underneath your needle plate, check your cutter. Use tweezers to remove any stray thread or lint build-up. Some modern machines will have a cleaning button which will move the cutter to enable you to clean it more easily. Check your manual to see if you have this function.

Firmware Updates

Firmware is a software programme used in electronic sewing machines. Manufacturers will release firmware periodically to ensure your sewing machine is behaving correctly. It will remove bugs and ensure your machine runs smoothly.

Firmware can be downloaded from your manufacturer's website and can be loaded onto your sewing machine wirelessly or with a USB stick. Check the website for any updates for your machine.

USB Memory Sticks

Some sewing machines have USB capability which allows you to download software, designs and firmware to your machine. It is important to know that your USB memory stick should be no larger than 16 GB. Larger-memory USB sticks find it hard to read such small files, and they may not show on your machine.

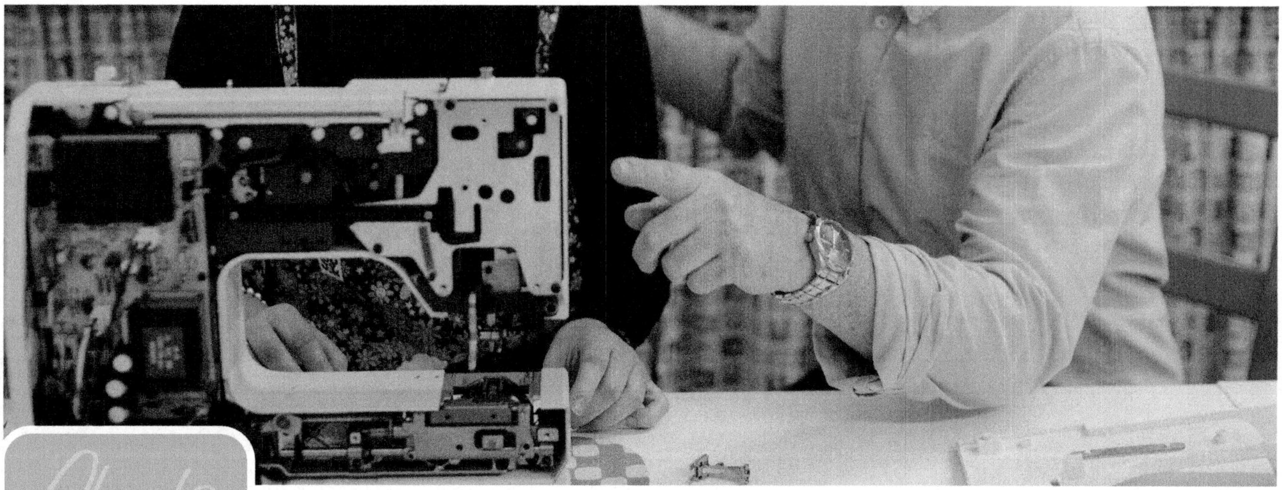

Chapter 13

ETHICAL CONSIDERATIONS

Ethical sewing practices involve mindful choices that prioritise fairness, sustainability and social responsibility. By embracing ethical considerations in your sewing projects, you can contribute to a more conscientious crafting community. Here are the key aspects of ethical sewing practices:

Fair Labour and Fair Trade

Choose brands and suppliers that prioritise fair labour practices. Look for products with Fair Trade certifications or those that are committed to ethical working conditions for their employees.

Sustainable Materials

Choose fabrics and materials that are eco-friendly and sustainable. Consider options like organic cotton or recycled textiles from thrift and charity shops to reduce the environmental impact of your projects.

Upcycling and Repurposing

Embrace the concept of upcycling, which involves transforming discarded or unused items into something new and valuable. This reduces waste and supports sustainability. Figures show that 85 percent of textile and cloth end up in the landfill. This is the second largest polluter on Earth behind oil. Think before you buy new.

TO DO

TASK!
Have a look in your wardrobe at clothes you do not wear. Can they be adjusted, or can you reuse the fabric to make something else?

Recycling and Proper Disposal

Dispose of sewing-related waste responsibly. Recycle fabric scraps or donate to your local scrap store.

If your sewing machine is broken beyond repair, consider donating it for parts which can be used to care for another machine.

Transparency

Be transparent about the materials you use and the labour involved in your creations when selling or sharing your sewing projects. Honest representation builds trust.

Supporting Local

Whenever possible, support local businesses and artisans. Purchasing materials from local fabric shops or artisans can stimulate the local economy and reduce the carbon footprint associated with shipping.

Teaching and Sharing

Share your sewing knowledge with others, especially those interested in ethical practices. Teach responsible sewing techniques and encourage mindful crafting.

Social Responsibility

Consider using your sewing skills to create items that benefit the community, such as sewing items for charitable causes like hospitals, for example.

Ethical Resourcing

Ensure that patterns and sewing resources you use are sourced legally and respect copyright and licensing agreements.

Mindful Consumption

Consume thoughtfully and avoid over-purchasing fabrics and supplies. Plan your projects carefully to reduce waste and excess material.

TOP TIP!
Consider having a stand at a local community sale or de-stash. Sell unwanted fabrics for other sewers to use. Our De-stash events at our shop are very popular with the local community. Consider organising one in your area.

Photograph by Sarah Hurja

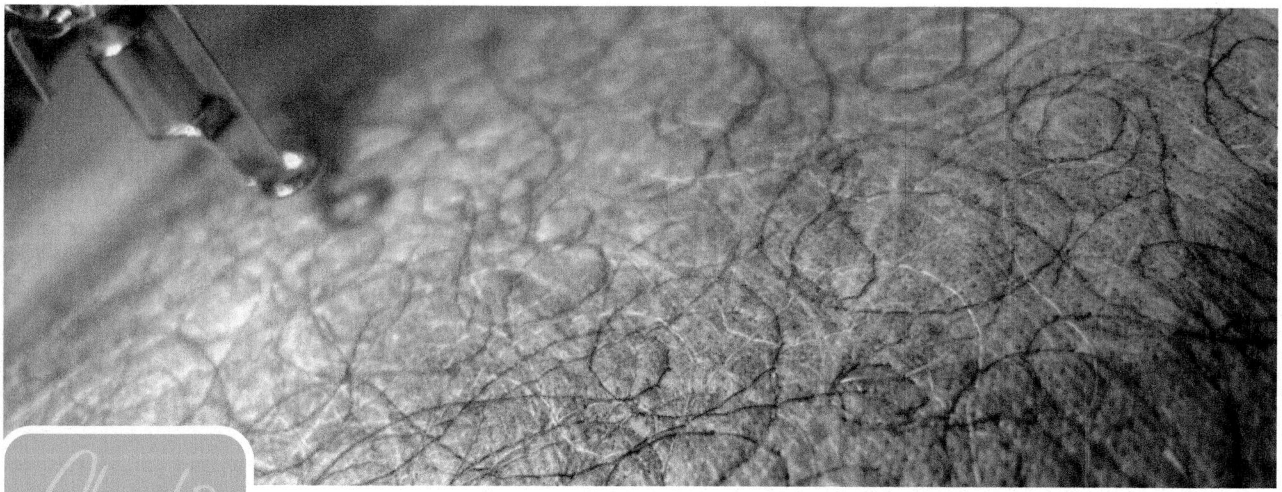

Chapter 14

A MINI PROJECT: REUSING THREAD SCRAPS

How often do we throw away ends of thread? Imagine how much you would have if you collected all of that thread and made it into a work of art or something useful.

Collect all of the old thread ends into a jar or pot and you will notice it mounts up very fast.

Make a thread bowl:

For this project you will need the following:

- A sewing machine
- An embroidery hoop
- A large amount of thread scraps
- Water soluble fabric x 2 pieces
- Thread
- A mould: you can use a bowl or something similar to shape the fabric

INSTRUCTIONS:

- Cut two pieces of water-soluble fabric to size, depending on the amount of thread you have. I would recommend having it at least 20 cm square.
- Lay your threads on one piece of the fabric in different directions until your whole sheet is covered.
- Sandwich the threads by laying another piece of water-soluble fabric on top. Put these layers into an embroidery hoop.
- Now stitch! This works best by using a free-motion or darning foot and dropping your feed dog. Stitch over the entire piece to join all the threads together. This can be done in any colour or different colours and in any direction. Scribble and have fun!
- Once you are confident that all the threads have been locked together, dissolve the fabric in water that is hot to the touch but not so hot that it will burn you.
- Gently rub each part of the thread to remove any excess glue in the water and lay onto a piece of kitchen roll. Dab the thread.
- Once the threads have all excess water removed, lay over an upside-down bowl and leave to dry for 24 hours. Alternatively, cover a polystyrene ball with kitchen foil and lay your thread over it. Pin on the ball in your desired shape and use a hair dryer to dry your bowl.
- Trim your thread bowl as desired.
- Finally, you could add trim or hand-stitch beads like I have, pictured below.

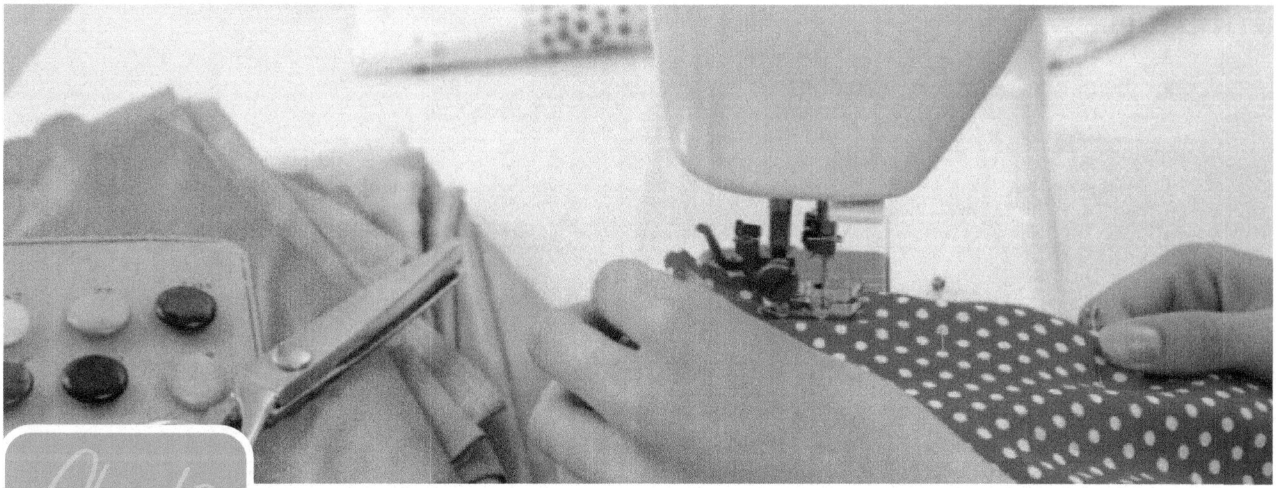

Chapter 15

PURCHASING A NEW SEWING MACHINE

When purchasing a new machine, there are many factors to consider. With so many sewing machines on the market, it is hard to know which one to buy. Follow these top tips to make your experience more pleasurable:

Brand

There are so many different types and brands of sewing machines that sometimes it becomes overwhelming. Brands from years gone by have now been bought by large manufacturing plants in China and do not have the same quality and longevity as they once did.

Some top-quality brands have become innovators in the sewing industry, while others have not moved forwards to modern times.

Firstly, look at the machine you currently have. What added features do you require that yours is lacking? Do you want to invest money into buying a machine which will last generations or just buy a machine off the shelf without even knowing what you'll get or how long it will last?

The key to this is research.

Budget

Think about the budget you have to purchase a new machine.

TOP TIP!
Always buy the best sewing machine you can afford at the time. You really do get what you pay for with a sewing machine. It is an investment, and you want it to be money well spent.

For example: If you spend £99 on a sewing machine, it may last you a few years if you look after it. The machine will be made up of lots of plastic parts. Over time, these wear. If you can afford to spend £500+ you will have a machine which will last a lot longer, and so on.

A sewing machine is an investment. I personally own sewing machines which are older than me, and they are still going strong and are some of my favourite machines I own.

Features

Look at the features of the new machine. Does it suit your needs? Is it too complex or too basic for your intended use? Do you require a needle threader on your machine? Do you want an in-built thread cutter? There are many questions to ask yourself before investing.

Hobbies

Take a look at your sewing hobbies to help you determine the features you require. Do you want your machine to drop its feed dog so you can do free-motion work? Are you just looking for a machine that will cope with heavier weight fabrics, as you like to make curtains?

Write a list with your top requirements, not just for your needs now, but also in the future. A machine should allow you to grow as you experiment with new sewing hobbies.

Where Do I Buy a Sewing Machine?

Purchasing a new sewing machine is a big deal. It is an experience in which you should be able to feel relaxed and not pressured.

Buying from a Sewing Machine Shop

Seek out your local sewing machine shop, and always read reviews first. You can do a little research online to see if they sell the particular brand you want, but if you are unsure, call ahead and arrange a time when you can get some expert advice according to your needs.

Always try the machine and compare it against other models in the shop. What suits one person may not feel right for another. Like a car, test drive it before buying. You could even take different fabric scraps with you to see how it performs.

Sewing machine shops often have deals on ex display models. These machines have had very little use and will come with a warranty. This could be a more affordable option if money is tight.

When buying from your local sewing machine shop, you will get full support and backup with your machine if needed. Build a good relationship with them, and you will always have the support, answers and tips you need.

Buying Online

Buying a sewing machine online may be your only option. If this is the case, carefully do all your research. When buying online, notice where the shop is based. This will save you lots of hassle and frustration later on if warrantied repairs are needed.

TOP TIP!

You will be responsible for shipping the machine back to the address at your cost. Sewing machines often don't travel well unless well packaged.

Always keep the original packaging for your machine in case of this. Some manufacturers will void the warranty if the machine is not in the original box it was sold in.

When buying online you don't receive the invaluable support you would get from your local dealer.

What to Avoid When Purchasing a New Machine

- Avoid buying from the place where we buy our food. Sewing machines from the middle aisle are often of low quality. You cannot "try before you buy" or ask any experts for help with purchasing. These machines are usually mass-produced Chinese imports, with little thought on quality and longevity.
- Don't just purchase the first machine you see. Research the brand and the model.
- Avoid buying from online marketplaces without trying the machine first and getting it checked over by a qualified engineer. As tempting as it is, I have had many machines come into my workshop which were sold as "working" when they are, in fact, broken and not repairable.

THINGS TO CONSIDER WHEN PURCHASING A PRE-LOVED SEWING MACHINE

Purchasing a pre-loved machine is a great way to be more sustainable. However, approach this with caution.

- Has the machine been serviced regularly?
- What is the stitch count of the machine?
- Does the machine look unloved/dirty?
- Is it running smoothly with no unusual sounds?
- Is the foot pedal working well and corresponding to your foot action?
- Does it have the accessories with it that you require?
- If electronic, are the buttons/screen working okay?
- Look in the bobbin area. Is it clean and free of rust?
- Does the motor sound okay? Is it struggling to start?
- Can you remove the needle easily?
- Are new parts for your machine readily available? If you are unsure, check to see if this model of machine is still being made.

TOP TIP!
Some sewing machine shops sell pre-loved machines. This is a good option if you have a stockist near you. The machines will come with a warranty and will be checked and serviced before you purchase—giving you extra peace of mind.

Chapter 16 SEWING FOR YOUR HEALTH AND WELL-BEING

One of the reasons I expanded my business into a bricks-and-mortar shop was to promote mental and physical well-being. After the isolating time of the pandemic and living with a chronic condition, I felt the need to bring my local sewing community together and make a difference in people's lives.

Since offering workshops and social events for all to attend, I have noticed a huge need for these types of groups. My workshops book up quickly, and my events are always a great success. New friendships have been formed, and new hobbies and skills have been learnt.

Many groups which met before the pandemic have never been re-formed. This is very sad.

TOP TIP!
Try searching for a local group in your area. If you can't find any, why not set one up? This could be a small meet-up in someone's home, a local cafe or even a hall.

Photograph by Sarah Hurja

Joining a workshop, class or group has many benefits. It offers a sense of community, learning opportunities, social interaction and the joy of sharing your skills with like-minded people.

Sewing is well known to offer a range of benefits for both your physical and mental well-being. Below are some ways in which sewing can positively impact your health:

Physical Health:

- Sewing improves fine motor skills, dexterity and hand-eye coordination.
- When sewing, you become more aware of your posture. By changing your posture during sewing sessions, you can help your back and neck health.
- The act of ironing, pinning and cutting involves physical activity which can help with your mobility.
- Reading and working from a pattern stimulate your brain.
- The concentration and activity required for sewing improve blood flow.

Mental Health:

- Sewing requires concentration, promoting mindfulness on the task at hand. This concentration can provide a break from racing thoughts and external stress, giving a sense of calm.
- The rhythmic and repetitive motion of sewing has been linked to stress reduction. Sewing activities act as a form of meditation, helping to lower stress levels and promote relaxation.
- Sewing serves as a creative outlet to express the way we are feeling through fabric, colours, texture and design. It is a powerful tool for emotional release and discovery.
- Joining social groups and classes is an opportunity for social connection, giving a sense of belonging.
- Dedicating time to sewing and putting other tasks aside is a form of self-care. Prioritising your well-being and engaging in a hobby that you enjoy brings many benefits to your mental health.

When was the last time you took a day out and worked on your health?

Some activities to help your mind . . .

- Go for a walk and seek inspiration from your surroundings. Look at the colours of nature, collect leaves and note the colours. When you return, find some scraps from your fabric stash and start stitching them together. Don't overthink about what you are going to do. Just sit at your machine and start stitching.
- Gather scraps of fabric, yarn and fibres and build them up in layers to create a scene of your favourite place that makes you happy.
- Never take on projects which are too large or overwhelming. A smaller project will give you a sense of achievement when you have finished it.
- Mindful stitching or slow stitching really helps drown out any noise in your mind. Work on a project slowly, feel the fabric, appreciate your time out and concentrate fully on the task at hand.
- If you are not a member of a group or don't have one in your area, join a virtual group on social media and get inspiration from other people. Seek advice, join in on conversations and share what you love to make.
- Sew with friends. Organise a sewing evening with your stitching friends. Being social can really help your physical and mental health.

Make a rope basket
First Sewing Social
Creative
Embroidery
Creative minds inspire

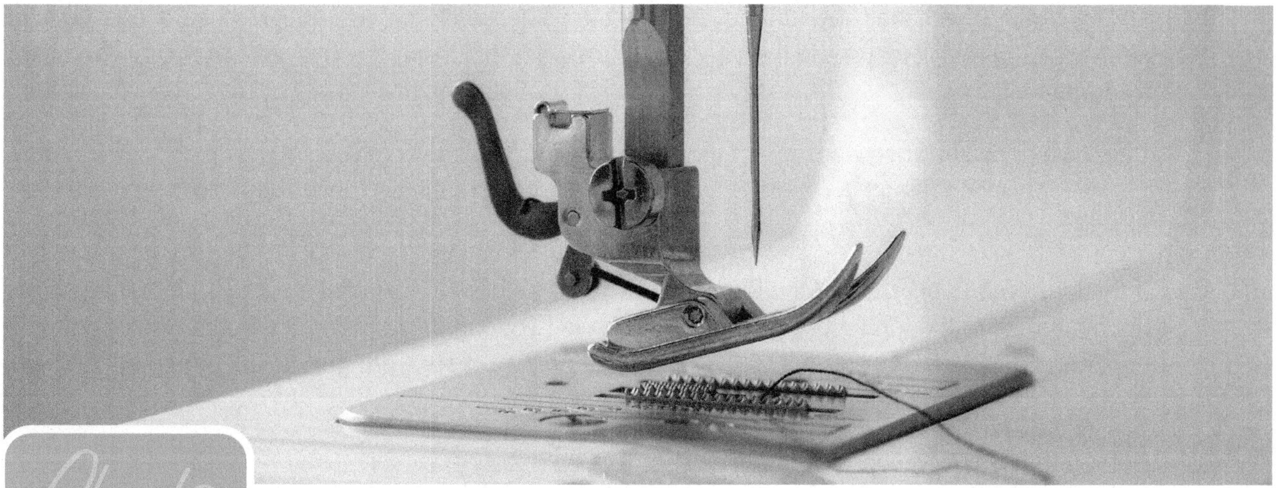

Chapter 17

TROUBLESHOOTING

There is nothing more frustrating than getting your project ready to sew and then your machine doesn't perform correctly. The following points are not an exhaustive list, but just some helpful actions you could try.

Always adjust settings and troubleshoot within your capabilities. If the issue persists, seek expert help and advice from a qualified sewing machine engineer or technician.

Thread Is Tangling Up Under the Fabric When Sewing (Bird Nesting)

01. Check that your bobbin is evenly wound and inserted into the bobbin case correctly. Check your sewing machine manual if you are unsure.

02. Remove your top thread from your machine and re-thread. Check that it follows the correct pathway for your machine, including any thread guides and, most importantly, the take-up lever. Refer to your user manual if you are unsure.

03. Your bobbin tension may be too loose. Extra thread could have unwound from the bobbin, causing a build-up of thread underneath the needle plate. Before proceeding, remove any thread build-up or loose thread you can see.

04. Try tightening the bobbin by turning the lower tension screw on the bobbin case a quarter turn clockwise. Tighten it, test it and then adjust until you get the desired results. See chapter 4, "Tension", for further information.

05. Check your needle. When was the last time you changed it? Make sure you are using the correct needle for your fabric and thread. A needle which is too thin for your fabric is more likely to jam than a thicker needle.

06. If the bird nesting happens at the beginning of your line of stitching, make sure you are bringing the bobbin thread to the top before you start, and leave two long tails of thread around 15 cm (both the upper and the lower). To apply a little tension and prevent them from getting caught up underneath, hold onto the threads before you start to sew.

07. Did you thread your machine with the presser foot up?

08. Have you remembered to drop your pressure foot before sewing? When using thicker fabric, it can easily be forgotten.

09. Is the thread you are using of good quality?

10. Clean your machine thoroughly.

Stitches Are Looping Underneath the Fabric

01. Re-thread the upper thread, making sure your presser foot is lifted. This allows the thread to gently guide between the two upper tension discs. Check this by lowering the presser foot and pulling the thread through the needle. If it has resistance, the thread is in the tension discs correctly. If you are able to pull the thread through the needle freely, the thread is not going through these discs.

02. Your upper tension may be too loose. Adjust your tension to make it tighter. Do this a small amount at a time. Does it make a difference?

The Needle Comes Unthreaded Before Sewing

01. Remove your needle and check that you have inserted it the correct way and all the way up to the top. Tighten the screw on the needle clamp to hold the needle.

02. Replace the needle for your appropriate requirements if you have not done so for a while.

03. Have you threaded the sewing machine correctly? Check that the thread has gone through the right path on your machine.

04. There may be a problem with your thread. Is it too thick for the needle eye? Is it shredding at the needle? Metallic threads are notorious for this. Make sure your thread tail is long enough.

05. Check that the thread is not caught on your spool cap or underneath your spool. This can sometimes get twisted and add tension to your thread.

06. Was your take-up lever in the highest position when threading? Turn your hand wheel towards you to raise it.

The Thread Is Fraying, Shredding or Breaking

01. Check your thread. Are you using old thread? Old thread fibres break down over a period of time, causing the thread to break and shred.

02. You may be using the incorrect needle for your thread. Is it the correct size and type for the type of thread you are using?

03. Your thread may not like your sewing machine. Some machines can be a little fussy on the brand of thread you use. Try another good-quality thread to see if it makes a difference. Poor-quality thread can have a big impact on your stitches. See "Threads" for further information.

When I Finish Sewing, I Can't Pull My Fabric Away, as the Thread Is Tight:

01. The machine is most likely halfway around creating a single stitch. Turn the hand wheel towards you to release it and complete the stitch. Now your fabric should pull away with ease.

02. Do you have a thread jam underneath? Remove your bobbin and check the compartment where your bobbin fits.

03. Your tension could be too tight on the top or bottom. Remove your fabric and pull on the bobbin thread. Is it pulling freely? Lift your pressure foot. Does the thread pull through the needle freely?

The Needle Is Bent or Broken

Bent and broken needles could be a sign that your machine needs some TLC.

01. Do you have the full needle? If not, you will need to remove your needle plate and use a pair of tweezers to get the needle out from the machine. Leaving the broken needle part inside the machine could cause damage to your bobbin case or further still the main raceway of the machine. Seek further help if needed.

02. Why did your needle break? Have you been sewing through very thick fabric? Using poor-quality needles?

03. Check that your upper tension is not set too high. This can cause the needle to break and the thread to snap.

04. Replace the needle and slowly move the hand wheel towards you. Is the needle hitting anything, or does it go up and down quite freely?

05. If your needle is hitting the needle plate, this could be a sign that your machine needs to visit an engineer. Sometimes, the needle bar (the part that holds the needle) can seize in a certain position or move out of alignment. This will need an adjustment.

06. If the needle is hitting something below the needle plate, do not force it. First check that your bobbin case is fitted correctly. If this is okay, then you will need to visit an engineer. The timing may need adjusting on your machine. Do not proceed with any further checks.

The Bobbin Case Is Jumping—Top-Loading Sewing Machine

Particularly when your machine has a top-loading bobbin (you place your bobbin into the top of your machine rather than underneath), you may notice your bobbin case jumping, making a noise or missing stitches.

01. Check your bobbin case for any damage. This includes needle holes, loose plastic parts or cuts in the case. If it is damaged, you may need to replace it or take it to an engineer who can repair it for you.

02. Clean the bobbin area and remove any lint, unwanted thread and dust. Place a small drop of oil all the way around the outside of your bobbin case. The part that comes into contact with the metal housing of your machine. Your machine may be dry, causing it to jump. Do not apply oil liberally. You will only need a small pinhead of oil.

The Machine Is Noisy

Try to determine where the noise is coming from. This can be quite difficult with sewing machines, as noise can travel. Always seek further help if required. If the noise is unusual for your machine and you have oiled and maintained it correctly, take it to your trusted engineer for further inspection. Do not continue to use it, as you may do further damage to your machine.

The Machine Won't Turn On

01. Check the plug on your sewing machine. Open it and make sure all the wires are firmly pushed into the small screw holes.

02. Change the fuse in your plug. A 3-amp fuse is recommended for domestic sewing machines.

03. Are you running your machine through an extension lead or power bank? There is a possibility you could have overloaded it.

04. Is the light working on your machine? If it has a screen, does it illuminate?

The Machine Is Running on Its Own

This is a common issue with older sewing machines. There is a high chance that the foot control has burnt out. This can sometimes be repaired, or alternatively, a new foot pedal will be needed. Do not attempt to do this yourself. Take it to a qualified engineer who can treat accordingly.

There Is Smoke Coming from the Motor of My Machine

Unplug your machine immediately and take it to a sewing machine engineer. This could be a fault on the circuit board, the motor or a capacitor which has blown.

The Machine Is Not Feeding The Fabric

01. Check that your feed dog is in the up position. There is either a lever at the back of the machine, a button on the side or a lever near the bobbin case that controls it (if your machine is front-loading).
02. Take your needle plate off and check that there is no debris underneath or caught between the teeth of the feed dog. (The feed dog is the metal teeth underneath the foot which feeds the fabric.) Use a dry toothbrush to clean the teeth and remove any lint or dirt.
03. Check that your stitch length is above 0. If it is set to 0, the machine will stitch in the same place.
04. If your fabric is still not feeding, check the underneath of your foot for any wear and tear.

The Machine Is Skipping Stitches

01. Change your sewing machine needle. If your needle is damaged or bent, it can cause your machine to miss stitches, or they will become irregular.
02. Use the correct needle for your fabric choice. See "Needles".
03. Always use a good-quality thread in your machine.
04. Adjust your top tension to see if there is a change.
05. Your timing on your machine may be out. Take it to an engineer.

The Machine Is Running but the Needle Won't Go Up and Down

01. Have you re-engaged your needle bar after winding the bobbin?
02. Turn the hand wheel. Is the needle bar moving up and down?
03. Has it been sat for a long time with little to no use? Your machine may be seized.

The Bobbin Tension Is Not Consistent

01. First, inspect your bobbin case for damage or irregularities. A bobbin case in poor condition can cause problems with your stitches.
02. Is your bobbin case clean and free of dust and lint?
03. Have you wound your bobbin correctly? Has it evenly filled and is it tight on the spool?
04. A bobbin tension adjustment may be required.

The Seams in Stretch Fabric Are Wavy

01. If your machine has a pressure function for the presser foot, adjust this. This will stretch the top layer of your fabric less, eliminating wavy stitches.
02. Don't sew too close to the edge of your stretch fabric. Increase your seam to eliminate this issue.
03. Use the correct stitch for your fabric. Using a straight stitch can cause the fabric to wave; using a stretch stitch will help your fabric to sit flatter.

The Machine Will Not Do a Zigzag Stitch

01. Check that your width button/dial is set correctly. If the width is set to 0, it will still do a straight stitch. Increase the width for your desired zigzag.
02. Is the machine doing other stitches okay? If the answer is no, the needle bar/width control may be seized. This can happen if your machine is not properly maintained or you only use straight stitch on your machine.

The Decorative Stitch Settings Aren't Working

Set your stitch to a straight stitch, then reverse. Is it reversing okay? Now try a zigzag stitch. If your machine is not doing these stitches correctly, there is a problem with your feed dog or width control. Take it to your trusted engineer for further inspection.

As previously mentioned, confirm your width is not on 0.

For further help in maintaining your machine, join me on my YouTube channel to watch my sewing machine maintenance video: ***@kbsewingmachines***.

Sewing machines can be very complex, and in some cases, their issues can be hard to diagnose. If you are in doubt or need any extra help and advice, please take your machine to a reputable engineer and do not attempt to take the machine apart, unless you know how to do so.

Thank you

for allowing me to share my passion and insights with you. I would like to invite you to share your thoughts, your experiences with sewing, the lessons learnt from this book and the moments of joy or challenges you have managed to overcome. By leaving a review, you not only express your own journey, but provide guidance to others considering this unique perspective on sewing machines. I would appreciate you leaving a review on Amazon.

Happy Sewing
Katie x

Photograph by Sarah Hurja

www.kbsewingmachines.co.uk
@kbsewingmachines
K&B Sewing Machines

SEWING MACHINE SERVICE RECORD

Date	Dealer	Sewing Machine Model	Repairs?	Serviced?	Next Service Due

My Notes

My Notes

Acknowledgements

With huge thanks to my launch team.

Benjamin Freeston
Carol Matthews
Anita Allen
Dawn Beaven
Teresa Barker
Louise Buse
Jane Duxbury
Susie Holmes
Sue Nias
Helen Westrop
Alice Wilkinson
Sandra Neil
Marilyn Stevens
Julie Apps
Niki Reynolds
Paula Norris
Natacha Pellicano
Carolyn Gale
Jenny Coffin
Jenny Beal
Jackie Kirk
Pauline Smith
Christine Down
Charlotte Ingham
Helen Poore
Penny Eames
Francesca Harding
Larissa Taylor
Naomi Watson
Alison Hulme
Linda Rondelez
Sara Travis
Julie Glasgow
Sasha Knott-Fancy
Mary Allen
Trish Gibson

Printed in Great Britain
by Amazon

36600632R00053